FREEDOM

TO ASCEND

JOHN GRDINA

ISBN-13: 978-1-956353-14-3 / eBook - 978-1-956353-15-0
(Published by Motivation Champs Media)

This book was printed in the United States of America.
To order additional copies, or bulk order contact: Motivation Champs Publishing www.motivationchamps.com

All Scripture quotations, unless otherwise indicated, are taken from the Holy Bible, New International Version®, NIV ®. Copyright© 1973, 1978, 1984, 2011 by Biblica, Inc.™
Used by permission of Zondervan. All rights reserved worldwide.

Scripture quotations marked (NLT) are taken from the Holy Bible, New Living Translation, copyright ©1996, 2004, 2015 by Tyndale House Foundation. Used by permission of Tyndale House Publishers, Carol Stream, Illinois 60188. All rights reserved.

Cover Design Credit: Chris Fabish

I've worked with thousands of people, teaching them how servant leadership can be applied to their life or business. Selflessness and love are the primary driving forces of this specific leadership, and John uses these characteristics so well in changing people's lives. The author truly empowers individuals to make decisions that put people first. Their daily actions cultivate results by letting go of doubt and despair to build small wins to live a fulfilled life. This book is a guideline on how to build or rebrand your world into something that you have always envisioned.

— *Howard Behar, President, Starbucks Coffee, retired*

"As an international mental performance teacher and ultra-athlete, Freedom to Ascend is a highly credible book for all readers. The content is sound from the experiences that John shares and the action steps that can be used to perform at a high level! If you need to transform your life, this book is for you!"

— *Brian M. Cain, MPM*

A great book for parents, kids, and anybody wanting to make a positive change in their life. If you are motivated to make changes in your life, read this book! Whether dealing with a challenging teen, a sassy co-worker, or just experiencing personal challenges, you will find "pearls" in these pages.

— *Gerard Daher, Chief Executive Officer, Speedeon*

John shares how his faith is the foundation of his life and motivates him to be a role model and mentor of others, not just in words but through actions. Using real examples, John shares his journey as a husband, a father, a teacher, a coach and ultimately as a mentor to those he encounters. It is an enjoyable read that will inspire readers to reflect on where their beliefs impact in everyday lives.

— Rev. John P. McNulty, D.Min, Pastor of Communion of Saints

This book clearly demonstrates how commitment to and compassion for others translates into building hope and direction in the lives of those who are finding their way or have become misguided. Viewing oneself as a change agent for the betterment of our youth is demonstrated in the stories told within the book, demonstrating action steps educators, counselors, parents, and community members can take to affirm others and fulfill the role of mentor and coach. From this counseling professional's view, the book is inspirational, motivating, and offers concrete action steps designed to encourage a positive mental framework that we can share with youth and others we encounter in life.

— Gail Michalski, LPC-S, LSW

I have known John for approximately two years now and one thing always stands out, his heart and deep desire to help and serve others. As someone that studies human performance and mental training it has become clear to me that we can accomplish amazing things with the right people around us willing to help uncover our highest true potential. John does a beautiful job of mixing his own experiences and the stories of others to unlock our Freedom To Ascend.

—Tim Douglas, Performance Coach, Speaker, Mentor

Life's Journey

One life on this earth is all we know,
So start living it now before you go.

For God has given you special talents and skills;
Use them with your passions and your life will be fulfilled.

Your attitude in life will also be a driving force
To wake up each day without remorse.

Though there will be times when the road is tough,
always believe in God and yourself
And those times will fade to dust.

Be kind, be patient, and love with all your heart
So you can build a loving family from the start.

Remember the choices that you make each day,
For they can lead you to a broken path or a promising way.

Now, enjoy life's journey for it will go fast;
Therefore, embrace each moment and make them last.

-   John Grdina

FREEDOM

TO

ASCEND

A guide to excel in your life and beyond!

John Grdina

Table of Contents

Dedicated to my wife, Megan, my rock and inspiration

and the beloved mother of our children

Foreword

When John asked me to write the foreword for his book, I was both very humbled and flattered. As an author myself, I understand the value when you ask someone to be a part of your book. With that in mind, it is a privilege to be a part of this book.

Although I have never met John in person, we have formed a connection and deep friendship over these past two years. As someone that values the importance of friendship, I am grateful to call John my friend. I would describe John as a lifelong learner. Someone that has a thirst for knowledge, and someone that longs to share that information with others.

I believe that we all have greatness within us. In *Freedom To Ascend*, John shares personal stories that will positively impact the reader. As a teacher, John is able to impact the students in his classroom on a daily basis. This book allows John's work to reach an even wider audience.

When is the last time you failed at something? When is the last time you set a goal and did not accomplish it the first time? I think life is all about growing, learning, and getting back up after we fall. This book is full of stories that will inspire you to keep going. Stories about people who have not only learned from those missteps, but they never quit.

One key takeaway from this book is our individual opportunity to have a positive impact on the lives of others. I challenge the reader to think about ways in your own life where you could impact others. What if we all tried to impact one person every single day?

I hope this book inspires you as it did for me. I hope these stories encourage you to get back up the next time you fall, and to go for your greatness.

We Rise By Lifting Others Up.

Christopher J. Wirth

Author, Speaker, Certified Mental Performance Coach and Podcast Host
Founder of No Quit Living, and The Positivity Tribe

Introduction

When outlining what I thought would be my first book, the focus was on telling the story of molding the minds of young adults. As I discerned what my mission was for writing a book, I understood that there was a greater purpose, one that touched more than just the mind. What I have discovered in my life is the power of the influence of the Holy Spirit, Christ, and the Father. The true source of my strength in my success is given to me every day by the Trinity. So the beginning of my journey of wisdom was understanding that it began once I opened up to having a relationship with the Lord.

This understanding—I call it an awakening—about how I can live with confidence and make an impact, was not always there. Growing up, I was a churchgoer and was raised Catholic, but I knew there had to be a deeper meaning to my faith than just showing up to the church. I had to experience the presence of the Holy Spirit to help guide me and help me in all the activities of my life. Once I realized that I cannot do life alone and that I needed guidance, support, encouragement, and enrichment from the Word of God, then I truly understood the righteous path for my life.

For me to be passionate about what I do every day, I have to understand my mission in life. This is my mission: to serve the Lord and imitate His ways while exhausting my gifts for His kingdom. All of us have gifts given to us which, along with our free will, are reservoirs for making decisions and positively using our potential.

For example, if a man is given a million dollars and he just buries it in the ground, he has wasted his resources. On the other hand, if a man who is given a million dollars uses it to live a life of influence and experience and to help others, then he has truly made use of this opportunity to have a major impact during his life.

This book is meant to tell the story of how I became who I am today, how my belief system guides my decisions daily, and the specific strategies I use to have an impact on others' lives. I hope that you learn how you can have the confidence and freedom to make decisions that positively impact you, your family, and your future family so that when you die, you know you have lived a fulfilled life that is truly rich with experiences and meaningful relationships.

The stories in this book derive from my experiences as a parent, educator, coach, leadership coordinator, ultra-runner, and podcaster. I include stories of students who had given up on themselves and thought they could not make a difference in their own lives, let alone someone else's. I believe by being positive, loving, and truly caring about those who walk into our lives, we can give them hope. These testimonies and stories serve as examples and inspiration for all readers to learn to build more positive and impactful relationships.

The book is divided by themes: The Beginning, Connecting with Others, Mindset, Strategies for Success, and the Conclusion. Under each theme, chapters focus on a specific message. At the end of each chapter, the **Action Steps** will give concrete and practical ways to incorporate these principles into your life and your relationships.

Putting all of these pieces together has been quite a process, but I hope that you will enjoy reading this book and that its message will help you impact others by being able to shine your light and influence in others' lives.

Sincerely,

John

Chapter 1

Who I Am

I would like to introduce myself to you. My name is John Grdina, and I am extremely passionate about helping others throughout this journey called LIFE. I love what I do, and I am grateful for what I get to do every single day. I have been a special education teacher for seventeen years in two different school districts. I have four beautiful children and a saint for a wife named Megan. Megan is also an educator. She teaches biology and anatomy in a suburban district on the west side of Cleveland, Ohio. Megan is a wonderful person, and if it wasn't for her incredible support, I would not have written this book. We have been married for fourteen years, and we live in Cleveland Heights, Ohio.

My life began on a snowy March day in 1982, in a small town off Lake Erie, east of Cleveland. I lived there for a few years, and then my family moved a little farther east to a new home in Concord. In that city, I enjoyed some of the best days that I had lived up to that point, playing football in the backyard with my neighbors and my brothers, hiking in the woods behind our house, and being raised by two great parents.

I was blessed with a loving family, support from my teachers, and great mentors in my life. From first grade to fifth grade, I attended St. Gabriel Elementary School, where I learned the Catholic sacraments and met many people who had an impact on my life. My mom and dad have been very influential in my life. Mom was a stay-at-home mother who later went on to receive her cosmetology license as a hairdresser. Dad was a painter who then became a facilities manager for the Brotherhood of Locomotives. They raised us to treat others with respect, to have character, and to love others.

As a young child, I played sports, did my school work, and always looked for new relationships. My outlook on life focused on being a good person and helping others.

When I was thirteen and my family and I had recently moved to Perry, I was in Mr. Logan's eighth-grade history class. Being a student in Mr. Logan's class was truly a joy; he told amazing stories about history and related them so well to all of us students. He had a way of making us feel valued. I told myself that I was going to be a teacher and a coach one day so that I could help kids.

On the athletic front, the coaches I had during football and baseball in middle school and high school also had a major impact on me. They built me up daily by teaching me to take responsibility, have a winning attitude, and give my all every time I set foot on any field. I decided I wanted to be like these great men.

My mission for my profession was set ever since these early years of my life. Throughout undergraduate work at John Carroll University and graduate work at Notre Dame College, I've continually strived to grow daily as an individual, learning new ideas and strategies to help others make progress in their lives as well.

My professional life did not begin in education but at a Harley-Davidson dealership, where I worked part-time after receiving my undergraduate degree in history with a teaching license in education. At the time, I had no experience on a motorcycle, and I had to convince the manager at the dealership that I would be a good employee despite my lack of experience. The position was a warehouse job, where I would be detailing and moving motorcycles daily. With my personality and positive outlook, I was able to make an impression and prove that I was the man for the job. Soon after, I would be riding hundreds of motorcycles and unpacking them off the eighteen-wheelers that arrived from Milwaukee, Wisconsin each week.

After a couple of months at this job, I began talking to a man named Jim about my being unable to find a teaching job. Jim worked part-time at the dealership, and he told me that he was a teacher at a career and technical school and there was an opening for an aide in a resource room for special education students. He advised me to apply and get my career started, even if it wasn't in the field of my choice. (I had planned to be a history teacher.)

I applied, got the job, and worked there for seven years with "intervention specialist" as my main title. During those years, I met individuals who helped me become a better professional and showed me what teaching is all about. At the career and technical Center, I not only served as an intervention specialist, but also as an internship director, job coach, career development coordinator for eighth-grade students, and co-teacher of a Technology Literacy course.

During those years at the career and technical center, I learned to become a professional. As a new college graduate, I was not by any means a polished educator. I had to learn how to form relationships and not rush into every opportunity by saying yes to my administrators. I also had to learn that doing small things right (paperwork, emails, lesson plans, etc.) meant a tremendously different outcome for all parties involved. Growing up in my profession came with some setbacks and lashes from not understanding how to do things the right way. My heart was always in the right place, but my techniques and strategies were not.

Leaving the career and technical school and coming back to my alma mater to teach and become the head baseball coach was a blessing. Even though it meant having a longer commute of at least forty-five minutes each way, it was a perfect time for transition in my life because I needed a change to grow. Coming back to the high school I graduated from was an opportunity for me to give back to those role models (coaches and teachers) who by their words and actions had planted the seed in me to become one of them—a tremendous influencer.

I would now have the opportunity to be a light in the lives of those students and players who needed hope, love, and a consistent daily commitment of positivity. I knew God had made this transition back to my hometown for a reason, and after being back for nine years now, I know exactly what His mission for me was: to help save those who thought they were hopeless.

I don't preach at school as an evangelist and never bring the name of Christ or God up in conversations. What I do is simply show love for others by imitating and emulating the love that God has shown me. I believe the best way to show God is to imitate how He would act, by simply listening to people, pouring love into them, and sharing wisdom from the Good Book.

The root of why I do what I do is founded in the love God has shown me. That is why I want to help everyone prosper, whether they be a student, colleague, friend, or newly formed relationship. I am on a mission to show God's love! I want every person I come in contact with to see this radiant light that cannot be penetrated by darkness because of the protection I have each day from my Father. I want people to be free from the bondage of hate, doubt, and deception and, instead, have hope for a beautiful future for themselves and their families. If I can be an agent of change for others and do the Father's will by showing His love toward others, I will have completed my mission in life.

Throughout these pages you are about to read, you will find stories from former students and friends that will help you learn strategies to use to be an intentional person who accomplishes more than you can now imagine. You'll learn how to be the light to others and how to find a deeper purpose in your life—a purpose that is more than just being financially stable when you retire and that gives you a reason why you wake up each day.

I am not a hero or a person who needs recognition from the stories, but I have had the amazing opportunity to be a part of bringing change to people's lives where many others thought there was no hope.

Rewrite your own life story now before it's too late, and experience the freedom to ascend in all areas of living your life!

Chapter 2

The Awakening

If you don't set a baseline standard for what you'll accept in your life, you'll find it's easy to slip into behaviors and attitudes or a quality of life that's far below what you deserve. You need to set and live by these standards no matter what happens in your life.

— *Anthony Robbins*

I stepped on the scale at my grandparents' house on Christmas Day in 2018 and waited patiently while the scale calibrated. After some seconds had passed, the digital reading came across. 175 pounds. For many, that may be an ideal weight, but for me, that was 20 pounds heavier than I had ever been up to that time. How could this have happened? Easy, I became comfortable. My wife had just given birth to our fourth child a few months earlier, and I had slipped into a routine of more eating and sitting.

That number, 175, stuck in my head all winter long.

A couple of weeks later, I was at my daughter's basketball game and sat next to Gerard, the dad of my daughter's friend. We talked about biking, running, and hiking. He told me stories of his 100-mile biking trips, a hike on the Camino de Santiago, and other adventures. I thought to myself: *What have I been doing in my life? I barely leave Ohio, I've been on only a few vacations, and I've become a plump five-foot-nine man.*

During our conversation, he advised me to read *Can't Hurt Me* by David Goggins. David is a former Navy SEAL, ultramarathon runner, ultra-distance cyclist, triathlete, public speaker, and author. That weekend, I purchased the book on my Kindle. **The fire was lit; I was determined to become a new version of myself. And everything changed.**

In February of 2019, I put an end to being comfortable on the couch, not exercising or watching what I ate, and not competing. The new standard became waking up early, running, eating better, and training to conquer my greatest fear—running a half marathon.

Since I was never a true runner before and only ran to condition my body in football and baseball, I had to learn how to become a more effective runner. Therefore, I set out to learn. I read books on running, specifically Hal Higdon, *Marathon: The Ultimate Training Guide.* I also watched an extreme amount of YouTube videos and learned many useful and notable skills, such as the Phil Maffetone heart-rate training plan, hydration with electrolytes, structure of a good schedule, and yes, caffeine, a runner's best friend!

In October of 2019, equipped with knowledge I had absorbed and miles of conditioning on the road, I completed my first-ever half marathon in Columbus, Ohio—with a great time. For those of you who don't run, that's 13.1 miles at a non-comfortable pace for almost two hours. It may sound like torture, but when I finished something that I had dreamed about doing for the past ten years, I had a great feeling of accomplishment. I actually laughed at the end of the race because it was not as hard as I thought it would be. **For years, I had allowed my fear to suffocate my dream, and once that race was over, I knew it was just the beginning of the new me.**

A few months after that race, I planted my flag in the ground to run my first marathon (26.2 miles). During the first few months of training in 2020, March rolled around and the entire country was shut down because of the worldwide pandemic. In early April, I found out that the marathon in Cleveland that I'd planned to run had been canceled.

Did I go back to the couch feeling sorry about a situation I couldn't control? Nope, I didn't skip a beat. I kept training, created my own course, and in mid-May ran a marathon. My family came out to support me, by either riding bikes or rollerblading. My brother James ran the last lap with me, and as we came to the finish, my entire family was there with signs, hooting, and cheering. I finished under four hours, was broken when I was done, and vowed never to run another marathon again.

But four months later, I ran another marathon virtually, then another, and completed the year 2020 by running the Bigfoot 50k, which had over 4,000 feet of elevation and thirty-one miles of treacherous terrain.

The year of COVID-19 didn't make me bitter; instead, it made me better. I finally got outside my comfort zone and accomplished things I never thought possible. I kept pushing myself to measures I'd never before reached. This all happened because I would not allow the fear and negativity to cloud my thoughts and inner dialogue. Instead, I chose to get better, train harder, and be a better version of myself.

How many of us fear something? If we're honest, most of us fear at least one thing in our life. The response should not be to run away from our fear but to run hard into that fear.

According to research, the most common fear is public speaking—it's even more feared than dying! Most people don't want to be judged or make a mistake in front of their peers and unknown individuals in the crowd. This fear is due only to our mind being fixated on how others perceive the way we will perform. Instead, take the mindset of "it's me vs. me."

Let me explain. We talk to ourselves constantly. That inner voice tells us that we are great or that we're a failure. That we've done well or we've blown it. That we are somebody, or we are nobody. People tend to worry too much about what others think of them rather than dealing with these crucial questions: *What do I think of myself? What am I telling myself?*

To develop a more positive inner dialogue, get out of your comfort zone and make gains in areas of your life. It doesn't have to be running; it could be reading more each day, reading aloud to yourself in front of the mirror to practice speaking, or taking that class you've been wishing you could attend. The more you sharpen the blade of skill, the more confidence you gain. When that confidence increases, fear recedes, and your inner dialogue becomes unstoppable.

To gain confidence, to have the edge in life, get uncomfortable doing something you fear or tackle a task you may not be good at. Once you do this, you'll be amazed at the way you feel and the moxie you'll show.

When have you moved forward into an uncomfortable situation in order to grow as an individual?

~ Think and Absorb ~

If you can't think of any instance when you've gotten outside your comfort zone because you wanted to grow, take time now to challenge yourself with an opportunity in your life. It could be going back to school to earn that certification you have always wanted. It could be running a marathon. It could be taking a course in public speaking. Take any negative self-talk and throw it to the wayside. Your ability to be successful and happy is based on taking risks.

The Gardener

Think of a good gardener. If a gardener planted his vegetables or flowers and then left them to grow on their own without any care, the results would be less than poor, reducing the quantity and quality of the produce. So the gardener is always outside trimming, weeding, and manicuring his garden. It takes consistent effort to produce a good harvest. This is how you should be taking care of yourself. **Start planting seeds where they will lead to growth in your life, and then tend those seedlings with intentional care.**

In the Bible, Paul talks directly to this point when he speaks to the church of Corinth. He states, "Remember this: Whoever sows sparingly will also reap sparingly, and whoever sows generously will also reap generously" (2 Corinthians 9:6). We must use these principles in our own lives.

We need to sow seeds of intentionality not only in our own lives but also in others as well. In Psalm 112:9, the author writes, "They have freely scattered their gifts to the poor, their righteousness endures forever; their horn will be lifted high in honor." To become a good gardener in life, we have to "freely scatter our gifts." This conscious act of selflessness will allow you to be lifted mentally and spiritually by attending to others' needs. Once you realize that you have the potential to be a gift-giver instead of always receiving, you will start realizing the beauty of how love really works.

But before you begin to nurture others, it is vital to understand how to nurture and cultivate your own growth. How can you do this?

First, surround yourself by the presence of the Lord by reading the Bible each day. Gain wisdom from understanding the prophets, the disciples, and the Son of God and how they shared the love for salvation through suffering and separation.

To truly understand how to be enriched as a person, feed on the ultimate Gardener and Creator, our Father.

Find a positive support system, people who can help as gardeners in your life. If necessary, find a mentor, someone you or a friend knows who has experience in the field of your pursuit. Start acting on a detailed plan and keep weekly check-ins with your mentor or accountability partner. An accountability partner will keep you motivated to complete tasks by constant communication throughout a day or week. This is a key component in my 40 Days of Deliverance program that I will explain later.

You may be asking, *Who would do this for me?* I am telling you right now, hundreds of people in this world would be willing to help you grow—you just need to ask. Find a class, join a group, and search social media or other platforms.

The Lonely Marathon

A run changed my network and gave me a mentor. I signed up for a virtual Livestrong race and, because we were still in COVID-19 times, I decided to run the marathon by myself in the fall of 2020 on the date of the Livestrong event.

On that run, I left my house at 5:00 a.m. and tracked my way down by the Chagrin River, passing horses in a pasture and beautiful farmhouses. Running, watching the sunrise, I was also listening to a *Three-of-Seven* podcast, which is produced by a former Navy SEAL, Chadd Wright. His guest on that podcast was Jeff Forrester.

Jeff talked about a book he had written at the beginning of the pandemic and explained how he had been deliberate about writing at least 250 words each day. He finished his book, *Unleashed Potential,* in two months! As he talked about his quickly written book, his story ignited a drive within me as I listened and ran. Since 2008, I have wanted to write a book. I had written a manuscript called *ABCs to Life,* but I never pursued publishing it because I thought it wasn't good enough.

All these thoughts of doubt crept into my mind while listening to this podcast but in my discomfort of running, I found joy—I would finish my book, *this* book!

I knew I had to talk to Jeff. He could help me finish my book in a timely fashion and get it into the hands of eager readers. That is when I made a decision that turned an uncomfortable situation into a rock-solid relationship in my life.

I hesitated to contact Jeff, but I did reach out through a direct message on Instagram. From there, we began a small conversation, and then I mustered up the courage to ask for his phone number to talk about a strategy to finish this book. He gave me his number, and now we connect every day via Instagram, text, or WhatsApp.

Taking this risk has led to so many more connections and opportunities. It created an exponential increase of relationships in my life that would have never occurred if I had given in to fear and held back from reaching out to Jeff. Asking one person I heard on a podcast to talk to me about writing a book has resulted in a growing network of people who have given me hope and a vision for a new chapter in my life. A simple action step propelled my relationships to a new level, and I have met amazing individuals who have impacted my life in a loving and supportive way.

Success and progress in our lives happen when we take emotions out of the equation. I believe in this mindset so much that I created T-shirts for all of my students and even sent one to Jeff Forrester as I helped him train for a 50k. The saying is: **Don't let your feelings get in the way of today's accomplishments.** We need to stop analyzing whether or not we "should" do something and instead, trust our gut and go after the result we so desire! Too many times, people mull over the "how" of what they're going to do instead of just doing it. We imagine and evaluate scenarios of possible outcomes. We overanalyze, and we're paralyzed and can't move forward.

A.S.A (Awareness, Strategies, and Action)

The simple way to get the ball rolling is the A.S.A approach—Awareness, Strategies, and Action.

Let's say you want to lose weight. You are AWARE that you are overweight. Good, now that you know that, you need STRATEGIES to begin to lose those pounds. These could be intermittent fasting, eating clean, increasing exercise, and more. The last step—which is the most difficult for people and the reason why results never come to fruition—is taking consistent ACTION on those strategies. If your vision is to lose weight, you have to have a non-negotiable list of what you are going to do daily and then execute the plan—no matter how you "feel" about it on any given day. Results happen when we take action and do not let our emotions be any part of the equation.

Too many times we overthink a plan and get bogged down before we've even started. Watching others on social media only makes things worse; we compare ourselves (never a good idea) to others, and try to match or outdo their journey, or make excuses why we cannot do what they've done.

What matters is that you get started and then stick to your plan. It's not about you vs. someone else, it's about you vs. you! Once you get started and develop small habits that move you toward your goal (like eating better and exercising, in this plan to lose weight), then you will start having results.

The worst thing you can do is to make your plan elaborate. Remember, K.I.S.S, Keep It Simple, Student. If you always look at yourself as a student in the game of life (and this is a much better perspective than addressing yourself as Stupid), you will make gains. Keep your plan simple. When you try to be a master and try to do too much, you'll be overburdened by the pressure you put on yourself and you'll most likely end up quitting.

A large part of the population is content to just play the game of life… and then die. What is the game? Get an education, get married, have kids, have a mortgage, pay off your mortgage, retire, die. Generation after generation follows the same track.

If that's the game we're playing, progress in some areas of our lives and our family's lives may happen, but not at the rate it could. We're too comfortable and content. Let me say that it's not necessarily "bad" to live a life like this. I believe having a relationship with God, raising a family, and making strides in our careers are all great moves. The only question is: Are we doing just the bare minimum in these areas?

We were designed for greatness and to envision an almost unimaginable life. Motivational speaker Les Brown put it best:

> The graveyard is the richest place on earth because it is here that you will find all the hopes and dreams that were never fulfilled, the books that were never written, the songs that were never sung, the inventions that were never shared, the cures that were never discovered, all because someone was too afraid to take that first step, keep with the problem, or [stay]determined to carry out their dream.

Don't let your dreams die! Strive to have small wins daily, build consistent habits, wake up earlier, achieve more, give more, love more, and push yourself to limits you never knew you had.

Too often, we tell ourselves that we can't build that business or influence millions of people or run 26.2 miles or even write a book. But we know deep inside our souls that we were meant to be great, so why do we quench the fire of these dreams? Is it simply too daunting to think of the work it may take or the risks that may be involved? Are we too afraid to do what it takes to succeed? These questions of non-action will haunt you to your grave.

What's holding you back?

Be bold; be great, and live uncomfortably to seek the desires of your heart before they end up in a graveyard. You were born for a purpose, to be a good gardener, to share your gifts with others, and to ultimately seek freedom in knowing that you lived out your mission in life. Therefore, don't waste your time and get started today by awakening your soul and all of its delights by doing good for others.

Action Steps:

- Set a date to do something on your bucket list that you've been postponing.

- Wake up on time.

- Create your A.S.A. (Awareness-Strategies-Action) plan.

- Create a daily non-negotiable list to build solid habits.

- To conquer fears and to grow, get outside your comfort zone.

- Go out, be bold, and punch your fears in the face!

Chapter 3

Be the Light

The people who walk in darkness will see a great light.

— Isaiah 9:2 (NLT)

My watch buzzed. I was at home after school, and when I checked the screen and saw a text had come from the mother of one of my former students, my first thought was that something had happened. As I read the message from my phone, her words caught me off guard.

> Just wanted to say Thank You for all that you did for Sam. She is thriving! Working as a licensed cosmetologist, she just moved into her first apartment! She is very blessed that you entered her life.

> I replied and thanked her for the kind words. I felt lucky to have been in Sammy's life, and I was so proud of her.

Her mother answered: *Your support made a huge difference. We are also proud of the young woman she has become.*

Sammy graduated a couple of years ago from high school. I first met her in my Foundations to Algebra class during her freshman year. It was apparent after the first couple of weeks that she disliked math—and school overall. Besides being her math instructor, I was her caseload manager and managed her Individualized Education Program (IEP) and interventions needed to help her make progress in her academic gaps.

The first year she was in my class, I learned that she hung around with a crowd who enjoyed extracurricular activities that were not positive. I worked with her on decision-making skills, trying to move her into a better environment that would help her grow, but even with direction from her parents, counselor, and teachers, she continued to make poor decisions. Her freshman year, with frequent disciplinary action and poor grades, was a blur for her. She entered her sophomore year credit deficient.

Sammy needed to care. To graduate, she needed to get her focus and grades turned around. How on earth was this going to be a possibility when it was clear that she didn't care at all about school?

I noticed that she loved doodling, drawing, and doing makeup. The lightbulb went on. I wondered if she would be interested in going to the local career-technical school for cosmetology. She had talent, but did she even realize that she had gifts to offer others?

Once I realized her talent, I got to work. I had worked at the local career and technical center and had information that I offered her about the cosmetology program. The program was two years long, and she would learn everything from cutting hair to makeup, and much more. The best part was that she would be there half the day, doing something that she might love instead of being "stuck" at school all day—at that, she was extremely interested! I told her that I knew the instructor well and trusted her so much that I had her cut my hair. Sammy couldn't believe this opportunity existed and she had never known about it.

I remember our conversation well. The path was not going to be easy, I warned, since she had to be at a junior status for her credits to be accepted into the program. She'd have to take online classes during the year to make up for classes that she had not passed. The idea of more school did not make her happy, but if it meant two years of doing something she was interested in, then she was going to put forth the effort. I talked with Sammy's mom and explained what Sammy would have to do, and she also came on board to make this happen.

I wanted to bolster Sammy's confidence that she had made the right decision in applying for the cosmetology program, so I gave her an opportunity of a lifetime.

"Would you like to cut my hair?"

"Are you serious?" she asked.

"Well, if you're going to be a cosmetologist, you should have some practice."

She didn't hesitate. "Absolutely!"

We set a time after school one day, and I brought my own clippers. My mom is a beautician, and she had usually been the one who cut my hair—until recently, when I began cutting my own and my boys' hair. I love the process and seeing the results of a "tight fade."

The day Sammy cut my hair, I invited the baseball team to come and watch. About twenty young men gathered around Sammy and her first haircut. She had to be terrified as I sat on that chair and guided her through the process of putting the guard on the clippers, cutting my sides, and finishing off with some snips with the scissors to the top of my head. As the hair began to fall to the floor, I could sense her nervousness. But by the end of the haircut, she was proud that she had done it. It looked great, and I told her so. I was proud of her for taking the risk to do this, especially in front of all the boys.

Days passed. I had been wearing my Brad Pitt haircut from his role in *Fury,* and Sammy had filled out the application for the cosmetology program and was waiting for a response. A letter finally arrived at her home. She had been denied entrance to the program and would be on a waiting list.

Sammy came in that day with a letter in hand, devastated. Her poor grades and credit deficiency were the reason she had not been accepted. I knew the cosmetology program always had many applicants; it was one of the most popular programs at the school. Things did not look good for her to get into the program.

No other programs so perfectly matched Sammy's talents and skills. I had to do something. I had to act on her behalf because I knew she wouldn't be *just* a cosmetologist—she would be a standout in this profession.

Since I used to work at the career and technical center, I had built strong relationships with the enrollment office. I called the enrollment specialist and explained Sammy's background and extolled her talent. I told the story of my haircut and how she had done a phenomenal job, but, more importantly, that I'd seen Sammy's passion for this craft. I pleaded the case that Sammy was not a typical student but she had made poor decisions and that's why she lacked credits. I explained that she was taking extra online classes and would most likely complete them during the summer.

I finished presenting Sammy's case by telling the enrollment specialist that Sammy *needed* to be in the program—she would be a shining light for everyone in the class, and someday, she would own her own salon. But it could only happen if she had this once-in-a-lifetime opportunity. Sammy needed this to change the trajectory of her life. I gave my best sales pitch because I truly believed Sammy would excel in the program and afterward, in the profession.

The enrollment specialist listened to my plea and reiterated that the program was always in high demand. I understood, but I persisted. I wouldn't have made the phone call if I didn't have a conviction that this was the best place for her, even though other students had the grades and better applications.

"I'll try my best, John, but I can't guarantee anything." She closed the conversation, and we ended our phone call.

There was hope.

A couple of weeks passed, and one day, Sammy came into my classroom. She was crying.

"I got accepted! Mr. G, I'm going to be a cosmetologist!"

I was elated to hear this news. Her voice held joy and even her expression had changed. **The darkness in her past was just that—in the past. She now had hope. She believed that this was the breakthrough she needed to have a purpose in life.**

Sammy was now on a mission to show the world how creative and talented she is in the field of cosmetology. She went off to the career and technical center during her junior and senior years and excelled! Not only did her academic environment shift, but her relationships also changed. She found new friends at her new school and began to make better choices. She wasn't perfect in all of them, but neither are you and I.

The important point from her story is that her mindset had changed. She no longer viewed her future as something unclear or foggy. She knew she had a calling, and she had seen the light of possibilities. Her talents were matched to a profession that allowed her to enjoy learning. And she was not only learning, she was also using her gifts to help other people look beautiful. There is such satisfaction in knowing that you not only make people look better by doing their hair or makeup, but you can give them a boost of confidence that makes them *feel* better.

This story about Sammy is a reminder that all of us can be the light to someone during their storm. The situation may be different than the education setting. Someone may be going through depression, fighting addiction, or suffering a loss. No matter what type of situation that individual may be in, you have the opportunity to help them change their path. Life is difficult for so many, but we have the opportunity to be the light others need.

How can we do this? By adhering to what the Word says. Paul stated, "In humility consider others better than yourselves. Each of you should look not only to your interests but also to the interests of others" (Philippians 2:3-4). We need to first of all believe that we can make a difference in others' lives and then never give up on people. This is how we show God's love for His people, by stripping away our self-interest and focusing on the well-being of others, showing them a path of righteousness.

We don't need a degree in psychology to help a friend who is struggling. We just need to be present and positive. With love, listening, and looking for ways to help them gain their confidence, we nurture others' self-worth and mission for being on this earth.

Increasing Your Light

But what if it's *you* who are struggling in a storm or with some darkness? What if your own life is difficult right now? What if you feel any light you have is pretty feeble—maybe even in danger of being extinguished?

None of us are all we can be. "Being" a light is not something we can switch off and on; it's a matter of who we are and how we perceive our mission in this world. So whatever our situation may be right now, how can we increase the light we have to share with others?

~ *Think and Absorb* ~

The first question is this: Who can help you move forward? Who can help you be more loving, more present, and positive in other people's lives? If no one in your circle of friends or family can help you, my advice would be to talk to someone in your community or a place of worship. Or—I offer this cautiously—find positive and loving people on social media.

All of us have the world of networking at our fingertips. Through technology, I've found a helpful connection that boosts my day each morning. This can happen when we use technology to put the right people around us. But what can be used for good often ends up as a mere distraction. Even worse, the world of virtual networking can plant impure and negative thoughts in our minds. We need to have the discipline to focus on how technology, specifically social media, can help us.

The Positivity Tribe

I recently met Christopher J. Wirth through a mutual friend, and Chris has been a major influence in my life. We connect daily on Instagram. His brand is called *The Positivity Tribe*, with a simple objective: to spread positivity everywhere. He has written two books, *The Positivity Tribe* and *The Positivity Tribe in the Locker Room*. His mission in life is to inspire people through positivity. He aims to spread positivity through other people's stories and in the books he has written. He speaks around the country, trying to help others apply lessons for growth and personal development. On his social media platforms, he also shares daily inspirational messages and quotes to encourage others. He has a motto that is very simple yet powerful: "We Rise By Lifting Others Up."

Chris is an inspiring individual. He posts positive messages daily on Instagram @no_quit_living and @the.positivity.tribe. A man of character who exemplifies how to live to the fullest, he is a source of light you are drawn to because of his outlook on life.

Chris speaks about the Positive Mental Advantage (The PMA), which is something he believes *everyone* possesses inside of them. The PMA is just like a muscle—it needs to be built, used, and strengthened. The PMA is not something you see; it's something you feel, believe, and put into action each day. It is not easy to always be positive, but it is very important. Chris shares this quote: "A positive attitude doesn't guarantee success, but a positive attitude guarantees you a much higher chance of success than a negative attitude will."

Chris preaches and lives hope, love, random acts of kindness, joy, and positivity. The culture he promotes is summed up in his acronym for the word CULTURE. Whether you are a student, teacher, parent, athlete, coach, or employee, I'm sure this will resonate with you.

Culture
Understanding
Love
Trust
Us
Relationships
Energy

I love how all these words play a part in creating and defining an environment that moves us forward in the right direction. Whether in your personal life, your family, or your place of work, these qualities applied in any environment will help to build a loving, positive culture. Who wouldn't want to be around people who bring these assets to the table each day? Do you embody some or all of these attributes in your life? Take some time now to circle any you think you need to work on in your life.

~ Think and Absorb ~

How can you be deliberate in creating a better culture around you? My advice would be to read a book on the specific words you've circled or follow an individual on

YouTube or your favorite social media platform who embodies those specific words. Start being intentional with what you think about, what you absorb from your environment (which includes your brain), and who you choose to be around you.

It can feel like the weight of the world is on your shoulders, but if you don't take action to connect with someone, read that book, or listen to a podcast or YouTube video and then move out of your comfort zone, your life will never move toward greatness and you won't be a positive impact on anyone else.

Another way to strengthen those around you is to live life with high-quality attributes that you can control daily. Chris presents this as a "7-Point Creed" for daily life.

BE Kind
BE Positive
BE Grateful
BE Encouraging
BE Humble
BE Generous
BE Forgiving

These seven words have the potential to change your life as well. Individually, these words are very powerful, but when all are brought together and practiced in daily life, they can make you an unstoppable force. Wake up each morning and state them aloud. Your intention each day is to be kind, positive, grateful, encouraging, humble, generous, and forgiving. Write them down in your journal or on an index card and keep them on you at all times to remind yourself how you can live a wholesome and character-filled day. Seeing, re-stating, and living out the 7-Point Creed, you will see your relationships with others grow and you will influence the culture around you.

Get started now and be a force of positive light to someone in their day!

Action Steps:

- Don't give up on people.
- Try to find one good quality in someone else.
- Praise individuals for their talents.
- Help someone by your words and/or actions.
- Seek positive influences for yourself.

Chapter 4

Connection Before Content

People don't care about how much you know

until they know how much you care.

— John C. Maxwell

Connecting with God the first thing when rising each morning and on throughout the day is the key to having the strongest eternal and internal relationship needed. Spending time in the Word, meditating on Scriptures, and then applying them in my life has made a difference for me in how I operate with others. Showing the love of Christ by listening, learning, and showing an invested interest in others' well-being is how I solidify strong and healthy relationships. I could never have learned how to do these things if it was not for connecting with God each day. Below is a story on how important it is to have faith, live in the present moment, and never take a day for granted when it comes to loving and caring for others.

On a May night in 2017, I received a phone call from the mother of one of my students. Two students from the school where I taught had been in a major car accident, and those involved had been taken to the hospital. Not too long after the phone call, I received a text from the mother telling me that both of the girls had died.

The two girls had recently graduated and were just starting their adult lives. Both were closely linked to me and my family. One girl worked at my mom's salon, and the other had been a student in my class all four years of high school. The day before the accident, the young lady who had been in my classes all four years had come to see me, but I wasn't in my room at the time. I told her that we would catch up another day soon, but that day would never come. It haunts me still to this day that I missed a chance to connect with her and will never get to see or hear from her again.

What I learned from this tragedy is that being present and forming true relationships matter. Attending the girls' joint funeral and crying at their caskets, I made a vow that if a student ever came back to see me or attempted to contact me, I would respond to them almost immediately. I never want to relive that moment of knowing that I missed being there for someone who was seeking me out, and now any chance of seeing or hearing from them again is gone forever.

How often do we go through life taking little moments with others for granted? Or we are not truly engaged in a conversation because we are working on something or replying to a text? Being distracted and wasting time results in less meaningful relationships. Not being present with those around you shows them that you don't care.

Therefore, how do we learn how to be more present and take advantage of the time we have with another? It's simple. Eliminate distractions!

I am a victim of such distractions in my life and have been working on using strategies to help me be more present and engaged with my family, co-workers, students, and whomever I meet during the day.

Strategies for Being Present

The strategy that has been working best for me is silencing my phone and only allowing notifications on my watch. I have found that if I do not use this strategy, I will unlock my phone to view the notification and then venture off into a spiral of distractibility.

At work, I wait until a break in my day to check my social media because the students and co-workers I am with during the day are my number one customers. When I come home, I leave my phone on top of the piano so that I don't touch it and become distracted. My family is a top priority for me and I can't have my phone become a wedge that pulls me away from spending quality time with them.

Assess your life now, and think about how your phone or other distractions may be affecting your presence with others. What are these distractions? How can you make a strategic plan to break away from them? Write them down on this page now so you can reference them later.

~ Think and Absorb ~

A True Commitment

Throughout my education, in all the classes offered in my college courses, I never had the opportunity to take a course on relationships, communication, or making connections with students. I learned the content covered by a course, and if relationships were addressed, professionalism was lauded over friendship. I agree that young and even tenured teachers should be taught ethics in their coursework, learning to trust their moral compass and to resist any temptation to form inappropriate relationships with their students, but making good and positive connections with your students is a vitally important skill.

We as teachers and mentors are sometimes pressured to focus only on learning standards, the pace of the curriculum, and end-of-course exams. We forget the importance of *relationships*. You could have a Ph.D. in any subject matter, but to not make at least one connection with your students is inexcusable unless you are teaching college courses with large numbers of students. Even then, building relationships along the way is important.

Look back on your own experiences as a student. Think about which teachers had the most impact on your life. Was it the ones who showed up just to recite their lesson plans, or was it the teachers who cared about you and asked personal questions to get to know you? Were they invested in you as a person and not just as a student in their class?

~ Think and Absorb ~

Try devoting the first part of the day—even the first weeks of work—to getting to know your students or employees, their backgrounds, their passions, and desires. Go deeper than simply learning to know names. Building deeper connections with them, you might find they have needs that you may be able to nourish. You may be able to fill the gaps of abandonment, help to heal emotional or physical scars, and ease pain. Of course, this deeper knowledge comes over time, but in all of our stories here, you will see that it took a caring connection to make a difference in a person's life.

People need to trust you and know that you would not do anything to harm them or take advantage of them. If that trust is built, people will be more likely to *want* to work for you because they know that you have their back. Even if the material they're learning or the job they're assigned is difficult, they know you care about their well-being.

Teachers, for example, need to sometimes put ourselves in the students' shoes. Most people can't sit for 30, 60, or 90-minute periods without a break or a way to enjoy each other's company. We need to be thoughtful of each individual and explore ways to build connection lessons into the day.

Make people feel important and valued, even if it's only in a sidebar conversation during a classroom activity or some friendly banter after class. As a teacher, presence is essence! Greeting students in the hall each time they enter or exit your classroom may seem insignificant, but it will have a major impact and give students increased self-worth just because you care enough to say hello. At work, do you sit in your cubicle or office, isolated from others? Find ways, however small, to make connections. As a leader, how often do you walk around to check on your employees and get a pulse of what is happening in your organization?

~ Think and Absorb ~

Commit to connecting with people. We all get busy and at times get lost in lesson plans (for teachers), developing, adjusting, and staying in survival mode with eight cups of coffee or an energy drink just to keep up the pace of our work and lives. But have a plan for connections. As a teacher, I prepare for teaching content, but planning and preparing to strengthen connections with my students is just as important. Preparation for connection usually ends up working in your favor. It is never a perfect system, but using a calendar to set up these activities alongside your curriculum (or job schedule) will help you maintain those connections.

We need meaningful relationships in our lives, and quality time is necessary to make the roots of those relationships go deep. Quality time allows people to learn from each other and to give hope to one another. Shared experiences and companionship build bonds of trust, which we all need as we strive to be the best we can be. Could we spend breakfast or lunch with a co-worker and get to know them better? Maybe go for a walk with a co-worker during lunch break and build each other up? We all go through trials and tribulations. Going it alone only makes the light at the end seem farther from reality. Sometimes, support can be given by just listening. Carve time out of your day to be there for someone, and be intentional as to when you are going to do this on a daily or weekly basis.

Life is about building long-lasting relationships, giving people hope through conversation, and allowing them to believe in themselves.

As a teacher, coach, and parent, I know that each person I meet in these areas of my life needs love and support, and I don't want to neglect any of them. How can we give quality time to develop deeply rooted connections with those in our lives?

~ Think and Absorb ~

Connections in the Classroom

During the 2018-19 school year, the math department (with the guidance and blessings of the administration) allowed us to take at-risk math students for one year-long class. I was a co-teacher alongside a colleague who had been in the district for twenty years. This was the first time she had taught a class consisting of many special needs students and English language learners (ELLs). I was fortunate to have co-taught for the previous seven years with this population, so one could say I knew what we were getting into. We'd be working with kids who had no confidence in their skills, hated school, and would rather be working a manual-labor job than be in an Algebra I class. We were up for a challenge, and we both knew it.

As we went into the year, we both agreed that we needed to shake things up each day. The class was 82 minutes long, and we would be teaching it for 185 days. That's 15,170 minutes!

Wait…

Here's a group of students who hate school and think they are dumb because most of them have failed or performed poorly in their past math classes and high-stakes tests—and we are going to put them in class for a full school year, hoping to remediate deficits and build on concepts for growth, for the end-of-course exam in May?

Yep.

It sounded great in theory, but we needed to forge new teaching methods to help us captivate their minds. To keep the students engaged, we used multiple online resources— Desmos, Edulastic, Kahoot, YouTube videos, and others. We also had brain breaks, when students could stand up, stretch, or play Simon Says. At the end of the year, we even played euchre to work on learning a new task, communicating with others, and using strategy to win.

The school year was chaotic at times, but in the end, the students took the end-of-course exam and their performance yielded the highest results they had ever achieved in mathematics. Our class had a seventy percent passing rate, which was a major increase from the previous year.

This may not seem like the greatest percentage, but the growth that occurred for almost 100 percent of the class was amazing. What was the difference? **These results came from building connections, trust, and relationships before pushing the content.**

This class was a clear example of how to make an impact in another person's life by connecting and caring. I always tell people that my students are my customers—they come first, and I have to do my best to ensure that they are improving not only in their academics but in their entire lives as well.

Time goes by so quickly, and we all—teachers, parents, friends, and family members—need to make the most of our time with the people we see daily, those we talk with once in a while, and even those we are meeting for the first time. Connections of caring will help all of us be more present, more authentic, and more influential in others' lives.

Action Steps:

- Be present and caring to everyone you meet.
- Reserve judgment and be a better listener.
- Be authentic.
- Show humility.
- Be present by putting down your phone.

Chapter 5

Life-Changing Relationships

For Builders, the real definition of success is a life and work that brings personal fulfillment and lasting relationships and makes a difference in the world in which they live.

— *Jerry I. Porras*

I received a text from one of my former players:

> You know, that's why I come to you with this. I understand you seem removed from high school crap, but right now in my life, all these decisions are major and I need your support and advice.

I retired early from a coaching position to spend more time with my family. I don't coach this player anymore, but I still talk to him weekly to see how he is doing with school and sports and most importantly, how he is progressing as an individual.

When I was coaching, we had a team creed: C.A.R.E. represented Commitment, Attitude, Respect, and Effort. All of these words have one thing in common—they can all be controlled by the individual. As a teacher, coach, parent, mentor, and leader, my job is to truly CARE about the individuals I am with daily. The presence I have with them is meaningful to me, and the relationships formed with students, players, or friends do not end when graduation day occurs.

The beauty of the dance of relationships is that they can last a lifetime, and the support and nurturing we both give and receive in relationships will have an impact throughout a lifetime.

One of my fondest memories is of working with a very troubled young man. He has a loving mother, but his dad was never in the picture. He hung around the wrong crowd, and he left our main campus to go to a correctional institute. This student was on a downward spiral academically, emotionally, and behaviorally. I knew he had potential if he could stay on the right path, and I never gave up on him. I visited him and wrote encouraging messages to him while he was away.

Following up with young people when they are at their lowest point is the most important action anyone can take. That's true in any relationship. When someone thinks they are worthless, a person showing up at their door at that exact moment can change their life.

When this young man's senior year began, he was not back at our main campus, but events in the spring of that year changed his attitude toward life—for the better. He came back to school, and his presence lifted my spirits. He graduated with the highest GPA he had ever earned in all his school years.

He asked me to make sure I was there for graduation day. I wouldn't have missed his big day for anything. After he received his diploma, we shared a huge hug, and someone captured our warm embrace in a photo. Later that day, he posted the image on Facebook and wrote:

> Couldn't have made it through high school without this man. He never gave up on me and he was the biggest motivation for me and he is a great guy and without him, I wouldn't have finished school. Thank you, Mr. Grdina. I care about you and love you. Thank you for everything, it means so much how you never gave up and were always there for me when I was having issues. One of the best mentors I could ever have.

His graduation day was amazing and gratifying, and the image of our hug will be engraved in my memory forever. He had been a lost soul who just needed someone who cared about him. He needed quality time, support, and someone who believed in him so that he could finally take the first steps of believing in himself. Without that belief in oneself, it's very hard to even get started in the right direction.

I've known many people who have lost hope and are just hanging on, trying to make it to the next day. Do you have people in your life who need someone to talk to or need just a small word of encouragement? What would happen if you started to build a bond with them, a bond to nurture and support *their* life and success? It may not be a student; it may be a co-worker or a neighbor or someone else whose life intersects with yours regularly.

As I was writing this, I paused long enough to text one of my former students. He had started a new mechanics program, and I wanted to check-in. He got back to me quickly and asked how life was. I answered *Great,* but I also told him that I was so proud of him for making a pivot in his life to better himself by going back to school and becoming a mechanic. He responded with a huge *Thank You!* It took less than two minutes out of my day to not just talk the talk but actually walk the walk. And that text exchange probably meant as much to me as it did to him.

Former students have written me notes of thanks. As a teacher and coach, it's a blessing to receive these notes at the end of a sports season or a student's high school career. I keep these notes by my desk at school—not as "trophies," but to remind me of the impact we can have on others' lives. They remind me why I do what I do and why I love to pour into people and help them realize the potential they have to be amazing individuals and strong contributors to society.

One student looked back at the hopelessness she felt at the outset of her high-school years, the difficult home life that had forced her to move out, and the lack of anyone who had ever talked with her about life and how to live it. Her outlook changed in high school.

> I just wanted to say thank you, literally for everything. I don't know where to begin. In my freshman through junior year, I didn't think I would make it to graduation. I didn't want to live through it. I didn't know what my future would look like because I didn't want one. You showed me that there's a light to the dark tunnel and pushed me to do work so I could experience graduation. I thank you for that. Despite all the times, I was a spoiled brat who didn't want to do her work. I thank you for never giving up on me entirely. I know I'm a lot of work. You don't deserve half the crap I put you through. I came from a broken home with broken trust. I came to high school not knowing the outcome or what to expect. Throughout all my breakdowns and bad days, thank you for being my shoulder to lean on and being the person to hear me out, to deal with me. The advice, the motivational talks will always be something I think about and return to when I face [life] on my own.

And there it is—as mentors, we are building blueprints in people's lives for their success in life beyond school. Our success is measured in *their* success.

One of Chris Wirth's facts for culture building (back in Chapter 3) reminds us that students will follow the actions and attitudes of teachers, especially if we have built caring connections with them. Who we are as people, as friends, as part of a community, influences our students—probably even more than the things we preach to them. That's why the principles we're presenting here are so important in our own lives—if we want to give our kids this blueprint for success, we've got to live it ourselves.

I was reminded of this when I read a paper that Kyle wrote for one of my leadership classes. During the off-season of baseball, I used "Leadership Thursday" classes with my players to help mold young men's minds into understanding that baseball was just a tool to create a sound character. I looked forward to these days and used many great resources from Brian Cain, Jon Gordon, and other successful performance coaches and authors. The class had great discussions, created goals, and built bonds for life during these sessions.

Kyle was one of my former players and one of the hardest workers I've had in my baseball program. The topic of the paper for the leadership class was "commitment" and why this quality is necessary to be an excellent player. He extended that to all of life. He wrote (in part):

> When I hear "Coach Grdina" yelled out in school or practice, I think of a man with no regrets. He lives his life to the fullest and tries to make other people around him better... From my first day in this program, you have

taught me how to be truly committed to something—you have taught me something that is one of the most valuable things in life—being a man.

He went on to write about looking up to me and how my passion for what I do has had an impact on his life.

Sentiments about you being a great teacher or coach are nice to hear, aren't they? We sometimes need that affirmation because there are some days we haven't made any progress or impact—or we might even feel we've lost ground.

But we *do* have an impact on others' lives. We can make a difference. Give your students or your athletes or your children or your mentees your undivided attention. Be an example of what excellence looks like, live with passion for what you do. Our lives influence people—in either negative or positive ways. Every day, the choice is yours on how you will impact this world.

Life-Changing Relationships

The positive and supportive relationships that nurture students during their high-school careers don't have to end on graduation day; they can blossom and be lifelong friendships. I've had former students help paint my house. (Don't worry, I compensated them for their efforts.) I've played golf and gone to baseball games with them or had them over for pizza on my front porch.

One relationship that has continued to progress over the years began a few years back. The first time I saw Nick was in the hallway outside my classroom. This kid looked like a problem. He was running his mouth to someone, and the glazed look in his eyes was one of a kid who didn't give a crap what you thought of him and who didn't care about you! He had confidence about him and an unmistakable air of street experience.

From that point on, I had small conversations with him whenever I saw him in the hallways. I asked questions like, "Where did you come from?" (He was a move-in.) "How is your family?" "How are your classes going?" As the year progressed, these sidebar conversations continued. I no longer saw him as a troubled teen and possible dropout, but as someone who could offer something to this world.

One day, later in the spring semester of Nick's senior year, I was approached by the assistant principal.

"I need to talk to you about Nick," he said. "I just had a conversation with him. He's credit deficient, and we told him his only option is to do online summer learning. We asked him what teacher he would like to work with, and he chose you."

I've never taught this kid, and I barely know him, I thought. And then I said decisively, "Sure!"

I'll be honest, I was taken aback. Outside of some small conversations we'd had, I didn't know this kid. For him to pick me was an honor. I must have said something or treated him in a manner that was different than he was used to. I have always welcomed the chance to work with students who may be challenging because they're "different." My mind was made up, and I was ready to get to work.

To get his work done and receive his diploma, Nick was required to come into school two to three hours a day for a couple of days a week. This wasn't so difficult for me since I'm a morning person and would already be leaving my house at 6:00 a.m. on those days to coach golf (which started at 7:00). Around 11:00 a.m., I'd head up to the school to work with Nick. This was my routine for a couple of months during the summer heat. My wife was on board with that schedule since it wasn't every day of the week. But we had a newborn at home, which meant my wife would occupy our other three kids with popsicles and slip-n-slides, while she tried to read on the front porch when our baby was napping. Sounds like a good plan, right? (My wife is a saint, so I got the approval.)

With self-discipline, Nick and I stuck to the plan all summer. During those days, we had great talks as I learned about his past. He told me that he had seen buddies shot to death, he had been stabbed and had done many illegal activities. Through our conversations, I was able to form a relationship with him, a true relationship that outreached any normal teaching responsibilities. We built a relationship of trust, which began by simply talking to him and helping him. He trusted that I had his back and that I would not leave him until the job got done.

To reinforce this commitment, I took a picture with him, made an eight by ten of it, framed it, and wrote one of my favorite quotes, "I will never leave you nor forsake you" (Joshua 1:5). I knew that Nick needed someone to believe in him and give him quality time. He's a smart young man who just made many bad choices. **How can a man or woman alter their course in life unless they truly are taught the basics of life that bear great fruit: love, compassion, empathy, time, belief, and choices?** We as parents, teachers, and mentors can't expect our kids to just "figure it out." We need to be the shepherds who help guide them to lives that prosper.

This guidance continued and grew over the summer. One day, I called my good friend and former colleague Ryan and asked him to come up and meet Nick. Ryan and I began our teaching career together seventeen years ago, and I knew he would love to meet Nick. Of course Ryan came, and the three of us laughed, listened, and just enjoyed each other's presence. It was a day I'll never forget.

When it was time for me to head back to my family, Ryan asked Nick if he was hungry. "Of course!" Nick replied. So Ryan took Nick out for lunch at the famous Checkers, and their conversation continued over the special Checkers Burger, fries, and shakes. Ryan called me later to thank me for inviting him to meet Nick. They had talked about Nick's past and how Ryan could help. Ryan said it had made his day.

That's the kind of guy Ryan is; he would drive to Alaska to give you his jacket if you were cold. He spent his time and money to help one of my students who needed more positivity in his life.

He and I still talk from time to time about how Nick is now doing. As of 2022, Nick is drug-free and working. I talk to him about once a month. He'll call me up just to shoot the breeze, and he's told me that he knows he can have an honest conversation with me. He loves the fact that I will listen to him and not ask for anything in return. I hope to continue to talk to Nick in the future, to build this relationship for life, to attend his wedding, and to hold his first child one day. I love that kid and can't wait to see what he accomplishes in his life.

These relationships continue to grow. I am still "here" for former students and players, and they have given back to me and my family. A couple of years ago when I was painting my house and texted some of my previous players, looking for help, some of them got back to me and were excited at the opportunity to help out. One of my former players, Matt, came out to help when I needed it most to finish the eastern side of my old colonial house. He drove out a couple of days to help me put on two beautiful coats to finish the job.

During the painting process, we had time to catch up on his life. He was seeking employment as a firefighter. He had recently graduated and was excited about his new career. We talked about baseball, relationships, and life. Those days together made me appreciate the good in people. Matt didn't have to come out and work for free, even though I offered to pay him. He did this selfless act because his former coach needed help. He also longed for something I always preached while I coached: unity, relationships, and teamwork.

Later that spring, I called on Matt again, this time to coach with me in my final season as varsity baseball coach. Matt came out and worked with the J.V. players, doing a phenomenal job with them. He is now the head J.V. coach at

Perry, leading a team of young men. To be honest, I don't know if I would have reached out to have him coach with me that spring if he hadn't come out to help on the house. If it wasn't for his selfless act, I probably would not have thought of him for the job.

I suggested to Matt that he join my leadership class on Thursday nights. I had my doubts that he would come, since it was with high school kids; but I had told him the concepts of the class applied to all ages, not just teenagers. Wouldn't you know it, Matt was at the very next meeting, and he's been there each week since. He wants to improve, not only as a coach but in the way he lives his life.

Life has a funny way of working out when you give back, and Matt deserved an opportunity. He took it and is now running with it. I am so proud of him, and we continue to speak regularly as I try my best to help him be his best as a coach.

Take Action to Make Connections

It is not only students who need people in their lives to support and love them. We do too! We were created to fill each other's cup, and in return, our cup will be filled to live another meaningful day.

How many times have you wished for someone to talk with who will not judge you for what you were going to tell them? Or have you wished for a mentor? If you do not have supportive, meaningful relationships, build new ones!

Many people out there truly want to help others. Never hesitate to simply ask a question of someone or tell them you are interested in getting to know them as a mentor, friend, or life coach. Find people who align with your values and then simply ask them for help or just talk to them. New relationships can easily be formed. The biggest hurdle to get over is to quit worrying about whether or not someone will get back to you or how you will respond to them. Just keep it simple and remember the reason why you are trying to connect—to gain insight and possibly form a new relationship to help you in your life.

Social media can certainly be used in the wrong way. But it can be a positive tool if you use it to connect to people who can help you become a better person. This is a recommendation only to be used if you are going to be appropriate and not banter back and forth. I have found it beneficial to surround myself with a small group of amazing people (on social media) whose values and mission are similar to mine; group chats motivate and help us in our daily lives.

It might sound crazy to suggest randomly sending a friend request to someone you've never met or to message them privately, but that's how my current close network of online friends began.

I listened to podcasts in a genre that was aligned with my core values and beliefs. When I truly liked the character of a guest speaker and connected with what they stood for, I'd reach out to them. Most people think this would never work—and it won't if you're trying to connect with most high-profile people who have millions of followers—but many successful people will answer your direct message. When they do, simply ask for their number or email, and you have just begun a relationship with someone who will be part of your new camp of friends. Before you know it, they are giving you support daily; they'll ask if you need anything, can pray for you, or invite you to special groups which they have formed or joined to better themselves and others.

All of us can be better at creating and holding on to great relationships. Life is extremely hard when you're doing it by yourself. Building strong relationships at home, work, and with family and friends is vital for your success.

Forging lasting relationships is a commitment you make to yourself and others. That's what life should be about—a continuation of nurturing and fulfillment in each other's lives.

Action Steps:

- Truly C.A.R.E. (Commitment, Attitude, Respect, and Effort) for everyone you meet.

- Be genuine and have character.

- Find ways to connect with new people using social media.

- Don't be afraid to ask someone you may not know well to join them in something you are passionate about.

Chapter 6

Fellowship

In your relationships with one another, have the same mindset as Christ Jesus.

— Philippians 2:5

This morning I went on a run with my running group in a balmy 13-degree weather. What motivates me to get up on a Saturday morning when I could be sleeping in? It's my tribe (Jen, DeQuan, and Samantha) and the power of fellowship and relationships that are built. During the run this morning, we talked about the importance of relationships and building each other up. Being present with each other in a common mission allows us to push and reinforce each other.

It may seem that running is just something to do for your physical body, but it's not; it's to improve your mental state as well as your soul. Running with my friends in the mornings allows me to experience a pure state of fellowship with no judgment or care, having open conversations that lead to restoration of the mind. It's an opportunity for all of us to decompress from the week and to understand what we need to do moving forward for the next. During these runs, we speak freely about things that are bothering us and ways in which we can do better jobs in our homes, as a spouse, and at our jobs. It's a therapy that cannot be replaced by anything else. It's an unexplainable way of learning together, and it would never be possible if we didn't make that choice to get up early and be with one another.

At the end of the run today, our conversation circled back to the topic of the power of relationships in our lives. We ended with a celebration of sorts. We had new T-shirts for 40 days of Deliverance, and DeQuan (a disciple in the program) and I took off our running shirts and put on the new T-shirts, symbolizing our relinquishing our past and transforming our bodies, minds, and souls.

I want to explain how this transformation can take place for *you*. Paul states in Romans 12:2, "Do not conform to the pattern of this world, but be transformed by the renewing of your mind. Then you will be able to test and approve what God's will is—his good, pleasing and perfect will." This transformation from the Lord takes place when you make a commitment to one another and listen to the Holy Spirit.

Prayer is essential to have a meaningful connection with God. In my life, prayer allows me to be guided by my Father and gives my life clear intention and purpose. This relationship that is reaffirmed each morning sets the table for how I interact with others in my life.

40 Days of Deliverance

How can a relationship with God transform your life? This transformation happened to me on May 23, 2021. God woke me up. I had a vision where I saw a Rolodex with the number of my followers on Instagram. The number went from a thousand to a hundred thousand to more than one million people.

I said to God, "Stop! I don't want a million followers."

He replied, "It's not what you want; it's my will. One million is not many; there are over seven billion people on the planet, and one million is like a penny to me."

I went to work that morning to mow greens on a golf course and listened to the *Order of Man* podcast. The host, Ryan Michler, said, "If you have a vision, if you have something that you're called to do, you need to do it now." I thought, *Okay, God. I hear you loud and clear, but what am I supposed to do?* He then laid it out for me while I mowed the grass. I heard "40 days" resonate in my soul.

The next day I went to work and wrote "40 days" on the board. I then stepped back and asked the Holy Spirit, "40 days of what?" After a couple of seconds, I heard the word, "DELIVERANCE!" I pulled out my marker and wrote "Deliverance." At home, I looked up Scriptures in the Bible and saw that there are so many instances where the number 40 and the word *deliverance* both occur, it was almost unbelievable.

Moses was in Egypt for 40 years, then he went to the desert for 40 years. It took him 80 years to do the Father's will the right way. He went back to Egypt and demanded that Pharaoh let the Israelites go (they were slaves in Egypt). After they are free, the Israelites go out into the desert and begin traveling back to the land God promised them. It took another 40 years to enter the Promised Land. In the New Testament, Jesus was in the desert for 40 days as well and was on the earth for 40 days after his resurrection. The number 40 occurs in many places in the Bible, but these are some examples of where the number has significant meaning in God's Word.

The first session of 40 Days of Deliverance was birthed on July 1, 2021. The program guide in a pamphlet given to each member reads as follows:

> It is with great pleasure to welcome you as you embark on a challenge that will help you as an individual. These next 40 Days will provide an opportunity for you to reflect, reset, and restore your life. The areas that we will focus on are our mind, body, and spirit. You will use proven strategies joined with discipline and obedience to help build structure and guidance during this journey. All of us will have an accountability partner and each other for support during these next 40 days.
>
> I ask that each one of you use this pamphlet as a way to be intentional in keeping the daily disciplines. Also, please journal each day or week as to what you are learning about yourself. Keep seeking the Lord and ask Him for guidance as to your mission, vision, and

goals that HE has in store for you. All of you have been given gifts from above; it's now a matter of how you use them to give Him glory each day.

We had a great first session, and many relationships were regularly formed for me and the other members of the group. One relationship I forged was with Bryan Scott, also named "Cornbread," from Dallas, Georgia. Cornbread had signed up for the program, but a couple of days before we were going to start, he told me through a direct message on Instagram that he wasn't going to do the program since he was going on vacation. I messaged him back and stated firmly that he *would* be doing it and that I would meet with him privately on Zoom to explain the program and how it works.

He started the program off like everyone else, with a forty-hour fast, and he said because of his discipline and obedience to God, he started to hear from God for the first time in his life. Cornbread was an alcoholic and stopped drinking on August 13 of 2020. He started the program weighing around 300 pounds. He explained that he had never built a relationship God or really got intentional about what God has planned for him. Instead, he was just going through life not knowing what true direction God had intended for him. When the 40 days ended, it was one year of sobriety for him! What were the chances of this occurring?

Our relationship kept growing, and a month after the program ended, we reconnected with a commitment to daily drinking a gallon of water and exercising. We then started a text group with my buddy Ryan, who I mentioned in the last chapter. The daily texts were a way to help all three of us become better people. We texted each day with pictures of ourselves drinking water and exercising. This continued through the rest of 2021, and it's been helping both my friends lose weight and get in shape while they're learning how to pray and connect with God.

Relationships are the connection all of us need in life. We can't go through life alone. Our connection should be with God each morning and end with Him each night so we can learn how to love others as He loves us. The word of God teaches us how to live like Christ, and if we can imitate Him and share meaningful conversations and experiences with others, we will be building each other up for life here on earth—but more importantly for eternity.

Teacup Theory

One day on a Zoom call to my leadership class, my friend Bree Hagen explained her "Teacup Theory" of relationships. She explained that as you grow as a person, you need to be aware of the people around you. Therefore, your circle of friends and family members you speak to may always be evolving.

She explained our relationships using the parallel of cups in a cupboard. If you open up your kitchen cupboard right now, there are probably three shelves. On the bottom shelf are cups you use daily. These cups you put in the dishwasher daily and put back on that bottom shelf. This shelf of cups represents the friends or family members that you talk to regularly. You may text them or call them and you know that they are the ones you lean on regularly. This shelf is your inner circle, and these people you pour your heart and soul into, and they do the same in return.

On the second shelf are the cups you use sometimes, maybe for special occasions when people come over. These friends are people you trust, but you don't talk to them every day. You know they're there, and you reach out to them occasionally, but they're not your everyday go-to people.

On the top shelf are the cups that you almost never use. Again, you know they are there, but they are not daily relationships. These individuals are not part of your day-to-day interactions, and you may have outgrown them. They are part of your contact list and you still want access to them, or you think you do, so they are not gone from your life. They truly could be someone you value but are not an integral part of what makes you the person you are today.

The teacup theory is very important. You should always be evaluating the cups on your shelves and reorganize them constantly based on what serves you at that moment. Sometimes you may need to throw teacups away because those individuals may not be helping you and your pursuit of progress in your life. It's not that they're a bad person, it's just that you have either grown apart or they have moved on from a relationship that used to be. If people would use this theory, they would make their lives less cluttered and create more space in their lives for the right people to help them become the best version of themselves. The teacup theory should also be applied to your social media, who you have as followers, and who you are following.

Remember, at the end of the day,

you are the average of your five closest contacts.

- Jim Rohn

Marriage

If you are single and looking for a partner to start a family, then learn the most important phrase, "Take care of yourself first!" This may sound selfish, but before you commit to a long-lasting relationship, you'd better have your house in order. How do you get your house in order?

Begin by gaining confidence in all areas of your life—career, finances, fitness, faith, and loving who you are. Start by having a steady job that will allow for stability in paying the bills. It is very difficult to attract a partner if you are jobless or constantly changing jobs. Having financial stability shows responsibility and allows trust to be built. Do not get into debt; spend only what you are making. Save your money and start learning this simple discipline early. Invest your money and have multiple "cookie jars" to pour into. The more you save, the better position you put yourself in for future purchasing power; or if something needs immediate attention, you will have resources on hand.

Fitness is an important factor because it allows for attraction. I fell in love with my wife Megan at first sight because of her beauty, and I am still in love with how she looks. We both make it a priority to maintain our physical body because we enjoy looking and feeling our best. When you are married for many years (almost fifteen for us), you constantly want to maintain or elevate your game of looking better for each other. Keeping up the physical attractiveness is not the end-all be-all, but it sure helps to suppress lustful eyes, which our weak flesh sometimes desires.

Faith is a foundational piece of your relationship with your partner. In Genesis 2:24, the verse states, "That is why a man leaves his father and mother and is united to his wife, and they become one flesh." When a man and a woman say their vows, they make a covenant with each other in the presence of God. They vow to love one another in sickness and in health, for better or for worse, ALL the days of their lives. Being centered with God's presence, living by the Word, and building each other up while loving as Christ loved us is the quintessential piece of having a rock-solid marriage.

Loving yourself is also essential for your marriage. It is impossible to truly love someone else if you do not love who you are and why God created you. If you question your purpose in life or feel that you need a life partner to make your life complete, you will be sadly mistaken about the result. You need to have confidence in yourself, love who you are, and know your mission as a person on this earth. Confidence— but not *pride*—is an extremely attractive personality characteristic. Neither a person who is a narcissist or one who continually lacks confidence in their life is an appealing possibility for a life-long partner.

And if you do have a spouse, there is no better way to have a strong marriage relationship than to learn from the writings of Paul. Paul's letter to the Ephesians states, "Husbands, love your wives, just as Christ loved the church and gave himself up for her" (chapter 5, verse 25). The word that comes to mind when reading this verse is *sacrifice*. Everyone wants to know the secret to a happy relationship and to start a family; it begins and ends with sacrifice.

Marriages will not last unless sacrifice is a part of the daily action by both spouses. In my relationship with my wife, I know that arguments or tension begin when I am focused on myself and not her or our family. If I am too focused on my mission to write this book or record more podcasts and I take time away from them, then there is not a sacrifice being made. There is a time and place for work, but it can't come before making time for my family.

In 1 Corinthians 13:4, Paul describes how to truly love: "*Love* is patient, *love* is kind. It does not envy, it does not boast, it is not proud." Therefore, be patient finding your partner in marriage, do not be prideful, and focus on loving with gentleness and care. Every day is not going to be perfect, since we are imperfect humans, but by sacrificing your needs daily, building each other up in love by kind words and actions, you will be on your way to a divine appointment with your spouse while you are here on earth.

Action Steps:

- Wake up and pray.

- Read the Bible each day to understand how to have meaningful relationships.

- Join a group or a program to meet new people.

- Have an accountability partner to help you become disciplined.

- Sacrifice your needs for your spouse.

- Love, be patient, and trust.

- Create a circle of five or more people who push you to be better.

Chapter 7

Attitude Matters

The only disability in life is a bad attitude.

— Scott Hamilton

As I sit here writing this book, I'm watching a young lady checking in books at a library. I just met her today, and as I watch her, I can tell that she is simply happy doing a task that many people might hate. She may continue to work at a library or someday pursue another profession, but her manner now toward a repetitious task is peaceful to watch. I wonder how she can be so positive while doing something that would be, for most, as mundane as watching paint dry.

For her and many others like her, happiness begins with an important start to each day: taking the stance of a positive outlook toward life's simplistic journey.

Yes, life's a journey. And I believe it is simpler than we think, but we tend to overcomplicate it. We'll make more headway toward our goals in life if each morning we can look at any challenge we face as a stepping-stone to our personal legend.

Teaching at a career and technical school and now at my alma mater, I have been blessed with experiences in two different types of educational settings. In my early years of teaching, I was assigned the role of Internship Director in addition to my teaching responsibilities. As the director of this program, I had the opportunity to give students experiences in the workday world of whatever jobs or professions they were interested in pursuing. I met managers and owners of companies, and as I listened to business people and learned what they wanted in their employees, I kept hearing about certain personality traits. Businesses were seeking people who not only had skill sets built for the trade but also could learn quickly and work well with others. Besides these attributes, the most frequently mentioned quality owners and managers valued was a good attitude.

One veteran manager explained to me that in all his years of experience, the common characteristic of the best workers he'd employed was that they had a positive attitude toward their job and life in general. These employees were well-balanced individuals who had a passion for what they were doing and would consistently look at the bright side of situations—even when something went wrong.

I see many students with poor attitudes toward school and life. Their discontent and negative energy radiate throughout the classroom and can rub off on others. If a student is in this state of mind, I always ask them what's wrong and why they're acting this way. They'll usually give me a response like "Nothin'" or "You don't want to know." Others will admit they're having trouble with their girlfriend or boyfriend. When a student is always in a bad mood and as a result has a negative attitude, I know there is something inside that individual that must come to the forefront.

Changed Attitude, Changed Outcome

One student I worked with recently seemed fine one day, but the next, he was angry at the world. His roller-coaster attitude was extreme. When I met him as a junior, he seemed to be a likable student who had a great work ethic, but if something or someone bothered him—watch out! He would f-bomb everyone and tell them to "shove it." He didn't care who he was addressing—it could have been the pope himself—if he was in the wrong state of mind, someone was going to get a verbal whipping. Yet I saw a positive light in this young man; deep down inside him was something of goodness and hope.

We got to know each other, and trust developed between us. One afternoon in the hallway, with no one else around, I asked him the reason for his verbal outbreaks and sometimes violent behavior. He explained that he was "messed up in the head." I told him I already knew that! I pushed further, asking what he thought was the cause of his "messed up" head.

Then he told me of his substance abuse. For over seven years, he had been doing cocaine and ecstasy and using marijuana. He described how serious the problem had become. The addictions were tough; he'd tried to quit several times but kept going back to the drugs.

It was clear that he was acting out during class because he was not chemically stable. I had identified the problem, and I wanted to work on a solution to change his poor behaviors and attitude in life.

We made a deal. I told him I would help him get a job if he would quit using drugs. He also had to attend meetings with other users in the community and show up every day at school with a willingness to work. If he relapsed and started using again, he would need to let me know.

His senior year was not perfect, but he did attend meetings, he received support from his family and his girlfriend, and we communicated daily about his progress. It wasn't easy for him, and there were days that he flipped out because an occasional buzz put him off balance. But at the end of the year and in the following summer, he took at-home drug tests and passed. He was so thrilled that he had accomplished his goal of being free from drugs that he called me to tell me the news. He applied for jobs and found one at a company where he again passed a drug test and began his employment. He was successful in achieving his goals because there were positive support systems for him.

We stayed in contact, and he recently called and asked if other students from my school needed a job. When I provided names, he recommended them to his employer, and several were hired. It's amazing that one year ago this young man was a constant drug user, and now he is working full-time, is clean, and is helping others. I'm so proud of him and his accomplishments. He realized that he needed to choose a path that did not require drugs, and he has changed his attitude and behaviors.

Attitude: Your Choice

One of my favorite quotes regarding attitude is from Viktor E. Frankl. Viktor was an Austrian neurologist, psychiatrist, philosopher, author, and Holocaust survivor. He wrote:

> Everything can be taken from a man or woman but one thing: the last of human freedoms—to choose one's attitude in any given set of circumstances, to choose one's own way.

To have the freedom of choice to choose one's attitude is profound, but how often do we blame external factors for our mood or why we feel a certain way?

Whether we are students or teachers, parents or mentors, employees or bosses, and no matter our circumstances, it is up to each of us to decide if we are going to have a good attitude about our daily lives.

The ability to see good things in our lives is basic to our happiness and success. Yet it's a difficult challenge for some people. This inability to see the good and to take a positive view of things may be due to genetics, a behavior learned at a young age, or just a bad beginning or break in one's life.

Choosing to have a positive attitude toward life is the only way to gain the freedom of letting go of negative thoughts and energy. Storms will come in life's journey, but we can hold the hope that the storm *will* end and the future can be even brighter. For everyone out there, I hope this book helps you understand the importance of your attitude and how you can shape it. For you adults who may be set in your ways, it's not too late to explore the possibilities of changing your attitude to one that allows for tremendous outcomes, not only in your life but in the lives of those you interact with every day.

The truth is this: Attitude is a choice, and it can make or break people.

If someone shows up to work being a "negative Ted," they're not likely to earn promotions, and they may even be viewed as a culture killer because of their stubborn stance on life.

Reflect on your childhood. Most likely, you did not have any problems or concerns at that time. The early years of grade school were exciting, new, and invigorating. New people and ideas were presented to you daily. No relationships to worry about, no money or work problems to deal with. Life was simple, fun, and interesting. I'm willing to bet that your attitude during this period in your life was positive and good, if not great.

How come, as we grow older, most people develop the opposite mindset? Is it because your daily routine is mundane? Is your partner in life boring? Is the government at fault for your economic status? A negative attitude finds countless excuses to have a nagging, neurotic day. When you choose to focus on the negatives in life, you will find them!

You may believe your attitude has been determined by your family, living situation, environment, friends, or things that have happened to you in your journey. Are you thinking that nothing good can happen now because of factors out of your control? Resist that thinking. The blame for your negative mindset cannot be put on someone or something else. No matter what happened in the past experiences of your life—or what is happening in the present—you now have a choice to decide, each second of the day, how you are going to feel about any person or situation.

Get your attitude straight, and everything else will take care of itself. You can change for the better, but it starts with a mindset that believes you can do so. A comes before B in the alphabet, and this same rule applies to Attitude—it must come before you can have a Breakthrough in any area of your life. Remember, every day must start and end with a positive attitude.

Being a teacher and coach has opened my eyes to what happens *to* people and *in* people daily. I've heard many students and players say, "I can't do this" or "They're better than me." Hearing these remarks makes me furious because they're already telling themselves that they can't achieve something. I wish I had a pocket copy of the children's book *The Little Engine That Could.* I'd remind those who have such negative attitudes that the little engine, who was undersized and carried a big load, accomplished its goal because it was determined and had the correct mindset.

One of the strategies I use when people explain to me that they can't do something is asking a simple question: "Have you tried to accomplish what you want?" If they say no, I encourage them to have confidence in themselves and try. If they answer yes, they have tried and failed, I tell them that failure is part of life, and if you truly want to accomplish a goal, big or small, you never give up.

"Well, I tried a couple of times and always failed. I'm just a failure." I've heard that. I understand that it can get depressing to fail at something you truly want. I have many times. Falling down is a part of life, and it happens. A driven person will get back up because they don't care how many times they fall—as long as they accomplish their goal.

I was blessed to meet a good man by the name of Jim when he came to speak to another teacher's class about setting goals and never giving upon them. In Jim's presentation, he showed a clip about a man named D.J. Gregory.

D.J. Gregory's story is a remarkable one. This young man had cerebral palsy, a condition from birth that kept him from walking. Doctors told his parents that he would never walk and would always be confined to a wheelchair. His parents did not want to hear this; they chose to believe there was a chance their son could walk someday. After many discussions with many different doctors, they found one who consented to do surgery to correct the boy's legs. The process was long, and there were more surgeries in the coming years, but D.J. worked hard and the passion to walk remained. Today, D.J. is walking with the aid of a cane.

D.J. couldn't play most sports, but he took up golf and began playing with his cane in his left hand and a club in his right. In 2008, he made it his mission to walk every hole every day of each PGA tournament that year. In the documentary, D.J. explained he wanted to prove to himself that he would be able to walk around 900 miles in one year. This was his goal, and nothing was going to stop him. The documentary showed footage of him walking the courses—including some scenes when he fell. The commentator asked him what he did when he fell. D.J.'s response was, "I know that I am going to fall, but I will always get back up."

D.J. will always need a cane to walk, but he accomplished his goal of walking by himself. Neither he nor The Little Engine That Could was going to quit—even when D.J. fell or the little engine rolled backward down the hill it was trying to climb. Both were determined, mentally tough, and kept their blinders in place so that they only saw the finish line of their dreams. (If you would like to view the story, go to YouTube and search "D.J. Gregory Story." Take five minutes out of your day to be truly inspired by this individual.)

The formula for success starts with attitude. Your attitude influences your journey toward your goal and the impact you can have to help others find their success.

Think of a successful or stellar person you know. What characteristics do they have? How do they treat people? Do they make sacrifices for others?

Now think about your personality. Do you find more negatives in the day than positives? Are you out there trying to help people, or are you trying to fill your ego? Is your life characterized by moral or immoral acts? When you fall, do you get up?

Again, **STOP** and think about these questions, and don't read on until you can answer them truthfully.

~ *Think and Absorb* ~

Now that you've had time to reflect on these questions, how would you characterize your attitude? What steps are you going to take to have a better attitude?

The first step I recommend is focusing on positives as soon as you wake up each morning. Know that you are here for a reason and on this new day you will find good in everything. Be thankful for a roof over your head and food on the table. Focus on the beauties of other people and the endless possibilities and opportunities in your own life.

Research has shown that people are less depressed when they wake up at a consistent time each morning. Also, when you wake up, DO NOT turn on the news. Take at least five minutes to read a devotional book, pray, or watch an inspirational video that will help you take a positive attitude before you leave your house. The more you try to focus on the good things in your life, the less likely you are to dwell on the negatives.

For example, find something meaningful—and positive—to do while you are driving to work, whether it is listening to music or thinking about how you are going to have a productive day no matter what comes your way. Preparing your mind to hold a positive attitude from the very beginning moments of the day will only lead to better outcomes.

I know that some people reading this might say, "That might be easy for someone else, but I tried that," or "It isn't going to work for me." I can't tell you what specific strategies to use to get into the right mindset every day, but I do know that you have to try something consistently for a while *with an open mind*—or nothing will work. If you tell yourself before going into meditation, reflection, reading a quote, or listening to music that it isn't going to work for you, well, guess what? It's not going to work. You've already made up your mind. Open-minded people tend to have more positive attitudes than close-minded individuals. Please, if you know that you are a negative person and want to work on becoming a positive one, then you have to be open-minded to new ideas.

What has worked for me? I wake up every morning around 4:30 a.m., read a devotional book and Scriptures, and pray. Then I exercise for at least half an hour. These early-morning routines give me undisturbed time to reflect on and gain clarity about my life and the tasks ahead of me that day. (*The 5 AM Club* by Robin Sharma offers insight on why many successful people wake up at this time and what they do to be in a "state of flow" each day.) On the ride to work, I listen to YouTube videos, audiobooks, and podcasts, or I pray or reflect on my life and what I can accomplish to bring growth in my life and, more importantly, in others' lives. I recommend listening to Jocko Willink, Jordan Peterson, Les Brown, *Positivity University* (Jon Gordon), *Three-of-Seven Podcast*, Steve Weatherford, *No Quit Living* (Chris Wirth), Jesse Itzler, *Order of Man* (Ryan Michler), *The Ed Mylett Show*, and *The Inspired Way* (Tim Douglas).

At work, I prepare before the workday begins, thinking about what I will be doing and how I will help students make progress in their lives. It's never easy, especially with students from different backgrounds and their problems, but I never give up on them. I believe I can make a difference every day, and that begins with my attitude. If I was a "Debbie Downer" with a negative attitude, my students would see right through me, and I could not have the impact on those students that I wish to have.

For any individual working with children, having the best attitude as often as possible is vital. I know that many of us can get beaten down by relationships at work or at home. It's tough. It is flat-out difficult to maintain sanity some days because of the outside forces beating on you. Les Brown would say that regardless of what hits you in the face, "If you can look up, you can get up." **You are going to have good days and some bad days, but how you respond to them when being around your kids or students is going to have an impression on them that they'll remember for the rest of their lives.**

You may not realize this, but your body language signals your attitude. If you're at work and you're short with someone or make sly comments to them or are being rude, they are going to tune you out—fast. If you don't think these days ever happen to you, just ask someone you trust at work if you are a good listener and are positive around them. Then go home and ask your family members as well.

We are not perfect human beings, but if we realize we're having a bad day, we can try to focus on being in the present moment and offer support to someone else in need. The more we focus on others, the more we'll find ourselves forgetting about our problems and not having time to worry about everything going on in our lives. Focus on others and their success. You may be surprised at what happens to you as a result.

Here's an assignment for you: Write down a couple of ways you think you could start to have a more positive attitude. (If you don't know where to start, use the Action Steps for ideas.) Pin this list up on your wall at home or at work to remind you to use those strategies every day. If you don't see progress with some of them, look for new ideas; keep searching until you find the right one(s) for you. This is a simple task, but it is a foundation for your well-being—and your success!

Don't give up on this assignment; see it through, because once you get going, you will be a transformed individual. People at work will be asking what's gotten into you lately and why you're so happy. Your spouse and kids will benefit; you'll be noticing all the things they do right instead of noticing what they do wrong. No one likes someone picking on them, specifically in a close relationship. **It seems that the more we grow together, the fewer compliments**

we give and the more nitpicking we do instead. This should not happen, but it does, because we get comfortable with one another and, as a result, expend less positive energy. With your new attitude, be proactive and complimentary, and tell others that you love them or that they look nice.

Take off your "Cruella de Vil" glasses and begin observing the world in a new light. Start noticing nature, your spouse, co-workers, and other aspects of your life with a new attitude, and begin living life instead of corrupting it.

Go now, and try to be the best person you can be for those who need you the most.

Action Steps:

- Be more aware of your attitude by reflecting on the words you use daily when talking to yourself and others.

- Gratitude: Wake up each morning, put your feet on the ground, and be thankful that you are alive each day.

- Positive Blinders: Stay away from anyone or anything negative.

- Clarity: Listen to positive and uplifting music, podcasts, or books.

- Be a positive human magnet. Focus on being someone people want to be around.

Chapter 8

Believe

Believe in your infinite potential.
Your only limitations are those you set upon yourself.
— *Roy T. Bennett*

One of my heroes is the legendary Abraham Lincoln. During the early years of his life, he lost three people he loved and had a strong relationship with. His mother died when he was nine; his sister died in childbirth when he was a teenager. Then, in his mid-twenties, his fiancée and the love of his life, Ann Rutledge, died in 1835.

After suffering the losses of his loved ones, Lincoln entered life as a lonely lawyer and then a politician. During those years of entrepreneurship and a start in politics, he failed many times. Defeats when running for political office included a failed run for Illinois Speaker of the House, senator, and vice president. Even with all of his personal and professional losses, he never gave up and believed that he was destined to do something great in life. At age fifty-two, after countless struggles and setbacks, he became the sixteenth President of The United States.

Like Lincoln, other iconic figures have known failure as well. Thomas Edison was fired twice; Walt Disney was also fired for not having enough imagination. Winston Churchill flunked the Royal Military entrance exam and finished last in his class. Elvis Presley received a C in his music class, and Michael Jordan was cut from his high school basketball team. I could go on and on about famous individuals who failed or whose ideas were perceived as far-fetched or ridiculous. The constant factor in each of these individuals' lives is that when they failed, they did not give up but believed that one day they would become great at what they did.

Think now about your own life and compare it to these many influential figures. Have you lost many close family members in your life, lost your job, or are in a constant state of depression? Well, if you have any or all of these conditions, you could be on track to be a major entrepreneur, entertainer, or even the next president!

You're probably thinking, "Yeah, right. I could never do anything great or become something special." Well, if you believe you are not destined for anything great, then the results will be just that—empty and void. If you believe and are driven to do something in any capacity, success will happen in due time.

Even when there are any losses or setbacks in your life, believing that you will get past those bumps in the road is the key to being successful. Everyone will fail; no one is perfect.

Expect losses, but learn from those experiences. **If you do not learn from your failures, no progress will be made; expect trials and tribulations with your mission, but never stop moving forward toward the goals and dreams you have in this life.**

Mindset Matters

Taylor, one of my former baseball players, was a perfect example of coming through failure to be great. In his early high school career, he was an average baseball player. He had passion but was not getting the results he wanted. From a coach's viewpoint, he was an average player but had tenacity and a good work ethic. Taylor failed to make the varsity team as a starter until his senior year.

During those first two years, he failed to be a great hitter, pitcher, and infielder—until he focused on what he could control and changed his mindset. As a coach, I knew that having a positive mindset and learning specific strategies would add value to a player's game. Therefore, I dedicated each Thursday in the off-season to teaching leadership from sports mental performance coaches. One coach in particular that I used in my classes was Brian Cain.

Brian is a former collegiate baseball player who helps athletes "master their mental game so they can consistently perform their best, overcome any obstacle, and stay focused under pressure." He has worked with hundreds of coaches and thousands of athletes to use proven strategies to improve their game. During my leadership course, with Brian Cain as a valuable resource, Taylor started to buy into this mental approach to take his performance to a higher level. He downloaded the mental pitching program which went through steps of how to control what you can control and live one pitch at a time. Once he began absorbing the knowledge of how to up his game mentally, the light-bulb switched on and he became a man amongst boys!

Taylor's entire demeanor changed. He was focused when he came to practice. He was now on a mission to live one pitch at a time, and to focus on winning each throw, swing, and ground ball. I remember telling him in one practice, "You look like an entirely new player." He simply responded, "I am."

Taylor was a new player mentally because he knew that every single action he performed was critical for his success. He knew that living one pitch at a time helped him stay present and lowered his anxiety about being perfect. He didn't have to "be perfect" anymore because he had unlocked the key of focus and presence.

This mind shift in Taylor created a player who would be forgotten by no one; he'll always be remembered for hoisting our conference banner in our gym. Taylor became our number one pitcher and helped us seize our first conference title in many years. He also helped as a middle infielder, bunting specialist, and designated hitter. A result of his performance was that the team gravitated toward his belief in his ability; and as a result, the team knew that we were going to win when he was pitching.

The lesson of Taylor's story is this: **Once you change your mindset to believing in your ability in every present moment, success will be your outcome.** It's not an easy process; change takes repeated mental and physical actions, but it can be done. If you want to take your life to the next level, as Taylor did, you need to apply specific strategies and not be afraid to work hard. It doesn't happen overnight. You can change your life in all areas if you want, but you have to be laser-focused and work consistently for better results. You also need positive coaches, friends, authors, and other circles of influence in your life daily. A seed (your belief system) needs to be watered (other people) and enriched by the sun (truth) so that you can grow as an individual.

There is greatness in each one of us, but it will not shine unless we believe in ourselves. Another word for belief is *confidence*, and it is vital for our daily lives. Do you walk around with a lack of confidence or belief in yourself? Do you wish you could be like someone who has great power or exudes great confidence? Are negative thoughts constantly crossing your mind?

~ Think and Absorb ~

Human nature is to make progress and find new ways to forge ahead. The reason why positive results do not happen for many people is that they do not believe they *can* have those results. This mindset could have resulted from repeated failures, or from always having felt like this from the very beginning of your existence, never feeling lucky or blessed. Well, I am here to tell you that if those are your feelings, you have given up, and your attitude and confidence in yourself are at an all-time low.

Now, I am not here to sugarcoat everything and say that you won't have failures in your life or get knocked down. As I've mentioned before, it has happened to me many times. What makes a difference, though, is whether or not we learn from those failures and setbacks and do not dwell on them. I always believe that my setbacks were meant to teach me something for the future. I believe that through my failures, I've learned either something new or ways *not* to do something. **I believe that in the end, I will reach my destiny.**

It is now your turn to change your mindset and believe you can do anything that you want. You just have to keep telling yourself that good things are ahead, and they will slowly be attracted into your life.

As I have mentioned, failing is part of life and it will happen. The important thing is to learn from our mistakes and bumps in the road.

Persistence and Prayer

When Megan and I said our vows on July 14, 2007, I knew then and there that our "perfect" little life was going to be wonderful and that we would soon begin trying to conceive a child. But after months of trying, we had no luck. After a couple more months had passed, my wife took a home pregnancy test and immediately told me the good news. We were both ecstatic, knowing for the first time that we were going to be parents. That was at the end of January in 2008.

Then, after some weeks had passed, she broke down and began to cry and told me that she had a miscarriage. The pain of watching her in tears hurt right down to the core. We went home that night and talked and prayed about how we would move on after losing a baby.

Megan and I continued the journey of trying to conceive, and months passed like a fleeting wind. She eventually did become pregnant again in the fall of 2008. We were both elated until one night, she felt immense pain in her lower abdomen. I took her to the hospital, where we found out she had an ectopic pregnancy, thus resulting in emergency surgery and another loss of life.

January 30, 2009, was the day of her surgery, a day I will never forget. With my wife in the hospital that weekend, I realized just how fragile life can be. Not only did we lose another baby, but I could have lost my wife as well.

Tears ran down her face as we drove home from the hospital. She was recovering and having to endure the pain of losing another baby, and watching her was emotionally painful for me. After I had her back home and our families were there for support, I had to remain strong and believe that everything was going to work out and that our dreams and aspirations to one day have a child would come true. It's extremely important to note that even though our dreams to have a child had not come to fruition, we never stopped believing that one day this pain would pass.

The pain did finally pass, and on July 4, 2009, while we were on vacation in Florida, she took a pregnancy test and it was positive. She and I truly believed that this time was going to be different and that we would in nine months have a beautiful baby.

Personally, I do believe in the phrase "Third time's a charm." On March 2, 2010, we had a gorgeous, full-head-of-hair little girl. We both were in tears after her delivery and named her Giuliana Rose Grdina. We could not be happier to have a beautiful daughter and finally call ourselves parents.

In two years, Megan and I had to deal with two miscarriages and months of not being able to become pregnant. Even though those were tough times, they made us stronger, and having a child became that much more important to us. "Keeping the faith" and never giving up hope is how we became proud parents of Giuliana and three more children.

For those of you who have a similar story and have or have not succeeded in your goal, do not give up faith, and keep believing that one day your dream will become a reality. The important part of this process is to keep believing. I learned that being a positive support person for my wife and praying for divine intervention helped us. Your strategy may be different from ours, but the foundation to attract what you want begins with believing in yourself, others, and a divine hand. Sometimes we cannot do things on our own; therefore, we must leave our ego at the door and trust in others to help us through difficult times.

Believing is the foundation for building all your dreams. You must believe in everything you do because confidence is the key ingredient for your success.

You are an amazing individual. All you have to do is believe in yourself and start taking steps to the vision you want in your life.

Action Steps:

- Expect failures to happen, because they will.

- Learn from others to help you grow as an individual.

- Pray for divine intervention.

- Throw out the toxic mental waste of doubt. Doubt kills dreams.

- Never stop believing, ever!

Chapter 9

Show Up to the Arena of Life

Opportunity is missed by most people
because it is dressed in overalls and looks like work.
— *Thomas A. Edison*

You've got to show up.

How many people in your professional career don't show up every day or are consistently late?

For the past thirteen summers, I've been part of the grounds crew at a golf course. I show up before 6:00 a.m. and have only been late once. When I first was hired, I mowed fairways; then I began walking to cut the greens and tees each day. This job, like most ground crew jobs, did not pay much, but it gave me both a quiet time for reflection and the satisfaction of a job well done as I cut the straightest lines possible on the greens or tees each morning.

I remember one morning early in my tenure at the course when two guys showed up two minutes late. Our boss reamed them out. When another worker said he was running late, the boss slammed his marker against the board and let everyone know the importance of being on time. "If you can be five minutes late, you can be five minutes early," he says. Being late was not an option; golfers were waiting to tee off at certain times, and if multiple people were late, it pushed back the start times, which in turn upset the members. We needed to show up on time, pay attention to whatever task we had each morning, and do work that met high standards, whether we were mowing grass, raking bunkers, or clearing the course of debris. Since my boss demanded excellence, we performed.

During the years I worked there, we've had a diverse crew, from high school and college-aged young people to retirees. Part-time employees from age 18 to 50 often did not work out well. Those individuals viewed the job as transitional, and as a result, they could not be relied on to be there each day or to perform at the standard needed.

To have influence and be a leader in your sport, your craft, or your family, you've got to show up every day. If practice starts at 7 a.m., you need to be there at 6:45. You should be the one who meets and greets others.

Showing up also means you have to be present in every situation. You have to lead by example. Do not complain, but embrace and lift others up each day.

Ryan, my former colleague, came to my school six years back to talk to my baseball team about the importance of leadership and being an elite person. He started the session by asking how many seniors were present, then how many juniors, how many sophomores, and how many freshmen.

"Freshmen and sophomores are looking up to the seniors for leadership," he said. "Younger kids gravitate toward what the older kids are doing. That's why it's important, on a daily basis, to set a good example, because these freshmen and sophomores will be seniors one day, and they will become the leaders of the program." Therefore, these senior members of the team needed to show up every day, setting examples in how they treated younger players and how they acted. Showing up means living your creed consistently.

You've got to shut up.

My team understood what Ryan was talking about when he compared suffering during conditioning for a sport to the same endurance necessary in a job. "When you're out there and you're training to get ready for the big game, your coach will have you running those wind sprints. When you do, you may start to feel some pain. Some of you may want to stop and give up. I'm going to tell you, those guys that go out there and push through the pain are the ones that you want to be. Those who make excuses and give in to the pain are the ones who also make excuses in other areas of their lives. They have a fixed mindset, an excuse for not being able to do something, and excuses for not achieving their goals. Achievers make it a lifestyle to push through the pain; they don't make excuses, and their mindset is always focused on their goals and desired outcome."

Do you have a clear view of your goals and desired outcome? Do you know where you want to go with your profession and your life? A good exercise to help you define your life goals is to create a vision statement. Write down some of your dreams you would like to accomplish. From that list, write a vision statement that explains why you are put on this earth and what you can offer the world. Post it somewhere that you will see every day.

Then develop a mission statement that supports that vision. Your long-term goals are your vision statement, but how you operate daily is your mission statement. What things do you want to do that align with your vision? (For example, how will you become successful, stay fit, and influence others positively?) These goals make up your mission statement.

When we have vision and mission clearly in mind, **excuses are useless** and they fade away. We get up every day and work toward these outcomes. When things don't go as planned, we see it as a challenge to overcome because we're going to work through the struggle to get to our goal. We show up, we shut up, and we get to work—because we're on a mission. We know where we want to go, and we know we alone are responsible for getting ourselves there.

Being responsible is one of the key elements of maturity. A true sign of growth in individuals is taking ownership of their work. They don't make excuses, they get the work done, and they have confidence in what they are doing. Being responsible also means showing up so that when you say you're going to do something, people can trust that it's going to get done. Taking responsibility and owning your work is maturity—a standard that has slid backward in recent decades because we want others to care for our needs.

As a parent, my mission in raising my children is to first and foremost teach them to have a relationship with God. Secondly, it's to guide them to becoming responsible individuals so that they can be positive contributors to society. They have to learn the independence of doing things on their own, without always having someone next to them to direct them. In essence, the true sense of responsibility is to get the results needed by taking the "ownership of work" approach, using the available resources and the communication needed to get the job done.

You've got to get to work.

Most of us show up to work. But *how* we then get to work is what makes great performance go beyond average performance. In his presentation to my team, Ryan talked about the absolute necessity of being an "elite person."

Most people just "go through the motions" in their jobs and their daily lives. They live an "average" life, doing only the minimum required, making excuses, arguing, complaining, and pointing fingers at others if things aren't going well in their lives at work or at home.

Only a small minority go above and beyond what their families or businesses need them to do. They are driven not by the minimum requirements but by true dedication, love, and selfless service. Thus, they show up early, leave late, and do not seek recognition for what they do because they know their mission in life requires going beyond. "You *have* to be an elite person," Ryan emphasized. In your job, skill, craft, and personal life, you've got to live and work to your full potential.

Just as cars may be equipped with a device called a governor that limits the maximum speed of the car, our brains seem to have governors that limit how far we push, whether we're trying to push ourselves to run a marathon, be an excellent welder, or be an elite teacher. Those limits may come from fears, negative self-talk, or even the desire to stay in a safe, comfortable zone. The governor of our brain can keep us from living to our full potential.

How many people aren't living to their full potential? The question for each one of us is whether we are living an average life, and if we are, why are we stuck there? Is it too much work for us to try something new? Is the governor on our brain blocking us from being an elite person in this world? Are we too comfortable in our lifestyle?

Comfort offers an easy path each day, but in the end, that easy path will leave us with emptiness and little fulfillment. Complacency grows in comfort, and complacency kills growth in our lives. It's deadly.

We get a job and put ourselves in cruise control until retirement. Many of us get up early and have our clothes ready to go the night before, but after years of the same routine, we let up on our dedication to our craft. Instead of taking action on our dreams and goals, we scroll social media to see what amazing adventures are going on in others' lives or to ingest the dopamine of "likes" on our most recent post. This way of living is how most people live, and our cup of feeling valued is left empty instead of overflowing.

As educators and professionals, how many of us are living an elite lifestyle? Does our love of what we're doing and our dedication to it drive us to sharpen our blade each day to prepare for our kids walking into the classroom or for the new client or customer who will walk through the door?

We need to stop thinking with an "average" mindset and start acting on our passions and drives in life. Being at the top is done by working through the struggles, not making excuses, and doing your best each day. Go beyond what's expected, beyond the "necessary." That makes you an "elite person"! That makes you respected as a person of character and gives you influence. That kind of "getting to work" brings success.

Life Lessons on the Golf Course

I've learned that small, simple things can make a big difference in my life and my work as they add value to my day—things as simple as waking up and going for a run, or sitting outside with my coffee and watching and listening to nature as the sun rises. On the golf course, it might be making straight lines when I mow or rake the sand traps.

My brother James also works at the course in the summer, and we'd always have a friendly competition to see who could lay down the straightest lines. Cutting and preparing the golf course each day, we use the same equipment and methodology as the most prestigious United

States Golf Association courses. We work to a high standard because of my boss, Brian Mabie, who was the former superintendent at Firestone Country Club. Each year he had to prepare, plan, and execute for the Bridgestone Invitational, which is a PGA event. When you have that type of professional standard, anything less is sub-par and unacceptable. He is a man who demands the best of us—to show up on time, do high-quality work, and leave a mark of excellence on the course for those who golf there each day.

He taught me a great lesson: "I try to hire character first because people with high character can be taught a skill. Just because someone has experience in the field doesn't mean they perform high-quality work or do the little things right."

Ponder that statement for a second. You may have a degree, a certification, or a title in your job, but does that mean you are a good employee or boss? The answer is no. To be a good worker, one must have a character with an exceptional work ethic. Those individuals work at a high standard because they care about what they're doing and how it affects those around them.

These "words of the wise" are true in any profession. It's easy to let our standards drop because society as a whole has become more relaxed in how it operates. **Our standards should never shift like sand; they should be the solid foundation of who we are as a person.** The quality of our work represents our family, our community, and ultimately, our country.

Continue to set the bar high by showing up, listening, and reflecting on what you do daily—and how you do it.

Action Steps:

- Show up five minutes early everywhere you go.

- Write your vision statement: who do you want to be and what do you want to accomplish in your lifetime?

- Develop a mission statement: what drives you daily to be excellent?

- If creating a mission or vision statement is too difficult, find one quote that you love and post it everywhere to encourage you to improve daily.

- Follow a couple of people who are successful and try to use their daily habits to improve your life.

- Don't just participate in life's arena, be a gladiator in it!

Chapter 10

Building Daily Habits

We are what we repeatedly do. Excellence, then, is not an act, but a habit.

-- Aristotle

If you didn't have to worry about getting to work on time, what would your morning routine look like? Would you sleep in? Eat a good breakfast and listen to the news or watch your favorite show? Exercise to get a good sweat in? Think about this question. No time restraint, no money restraint, what would you do?

The answer to this question is so important because your morning routines jump-start your day to your success. I have learned to have a daily routine; I need to do little things right each morning. Each day I get up around the same time, between: 4:30 and 5:00 a.m. I pray immediately upon waking up, no phone, just being present with God. I proceed to exercise for at least thirty minutes, then clean up, help my family get ready, and get out to conquer the day. These daily habits are imperative; a non-negotiable schedule creates a mindset that I have won the day before the day has started. I could go into the science and research that supports this experience of meditation and exercise creating strong physical and emotional wellness, but I'm here to tell you in simple words, it works!

What you hear and see first each morning can truly alter the course of your day. Building daily habits of waking up on time and listening to positive messages is key to starting the day off right, and starting the day off right sets the stage for you to have a positive impact on your own life and others' lives throughout the day.

Another habit that has many benefits is the habit of working hard at everything you do. Your relationships, business, and personal growth will all see positive results if this is a daily habit. Working hard simply means putting in more time with something because you want to make progress. **If the habit of hard work is not the bedrock for your daily operations, you are drifting down the river of comfort—and you'll see little to zero results.**

Changed Mindset + Small Habits = Success

Nate, one of my students, transformed his life during his high school years by changing his habits. I coached him as a freshman and sophomore in baseball. He was a very athletic young man who had loads of potential. As a sophomore, he started on varsity as an outfielder but was also a spot reliever as a pitcher. He was raw, but he had passion. Due to the

COVID-19 pandemic, he did not play high school ball during his junior year, but he did play summer baseball on competitive teams after both his sophomore and junior years. Coming into his senior year, he participated in my weekly leadership class.

Throughout his senior year, he was more focused and driven. He participated in weekly Zoom calls, read self-help books, and created a personalized vision plan. We talked throughout the year, conversations about school, working out, baseball, and his relationships with family and girlfriends. I wanted to help him become the best person he could be. I even bought him a journal to write down his plan each day and reflect on how he was moving forward with his vision and life plan. Coaching and his discipline and hard work resulted in his breaking the school's strikeout record and pitching one of the best seasons that I can recall from any high school student-athlete.

I asked Nate recently about things he's done that have helped him to be successful. Here are some of his thoughts:

> I started where a lot of people believe they are—on top of the world. But that's a false reality for many people. We create false realities—lie to ourselves—because we are afraid of the truth. We're afraid of what is going on. Facing the truth isn't always easy. But lying to yourself will always get you to the same destination in life—the bottom.

I learned to create my self-worth. I'd tell myself every day to trust myself, love myself, and care for myself in every way that I'd ask for someone else to trust, love, and care for me. Doing this showed me that certain things I was doing and people I was building relationships with were not worth my time.

I also studied the Law of Attraction, which is basically that you reap what you sow. If you think it, believe it, and then speak it, it will come to light. This may be the biggest piece in my journey to success. Positivity attracts positivity, while negativity attracts negativity.

You attract what you seek. If you want great things, then you first must be a great person who does great things so regularly that it becomes ordinary. I never complained after failing, I simply told myself that I need to be greater and that I wasn't doing enough. Then I went and did more than enough.

Nate changed his mindset, habits, and rules of how he lives. As a result, he is getting the desired outcomes and achieving at a high level.

To be superior at anything in life, you have to have a vision and then take action on that vision while canceling all the distractions around you.

What might you need to change in your life to be great?

~ Think and Absorb ~

Start Small

My friend Jeff Forrester, who you met in Chapter 2 ("The Awakening"), joined me on my podcast, *The John Grdina Classroom,* Episode 2, and talked about improving our lives by breaking down the goals we have set. Jeff has been running for almost ten years, and for the past two years, I have created a 50k race plan for him. He explained that having a plan that will take three to four months may seem daunting, but if he could just stick to the plan for *each day,* in the end, he would have success.

When we talked about faith, Jeff applied the same principle to improving our relationship with God. "Small" and "consistent" lead to big impacts. He explained:

> If you are new to the faith or have a renewed desire to walk with Jesus and have a stronger faith, the best plan is to start small. Both physically and spiritually, starting small has had a big impact for me. Start with just opening the YouVersion Bible app and reading the Bible verse on your phone. Just short and sweet, just one verse a day. Be consistent with it, and be an active participant in your walk. You can't be a passive Christian, just like you can't be a

passive runner. Just like you made me an awesome 50k plan, but if it's just taped to the wall and I don't follow it, I'm not going to grow and become a better runner. The plan for spiritual strength for Christians is to follow the Bible, and if you don't read the Bible, you won't have a guide to lead you in your life, and don't have a true relationship with God.

As Jeff and I continued our conversation, he explained that over the past three years, consistent study of Scripture has allowed him to trust God more and see breakthroughs in his life. These breakthroughs have been listening to God, getting in the Word for longer periods of time, and being an active participant in what the Bible teaches. He has also been more aware of sins and is minimizing them daily. Lastly, Jeff says this discipline of waking up each morning and being obedient to God in studying the Word has made his relationships with his wife and friends richer than he ever imagined.

Jeff stated firmly that God has been directing him to continue to be in His Word. He read Isaiah 40:8, "The grass withers and the flowers fall, but the word of our God endures forever." Jeff explained that you don't have to be an expert in all of the Bible to strengthen your relationship with God; just start reading one verse a day. Being consistent with this plan, Jeff is now going further than just one verse per day and is reading deeper into the books of the Bible. The strategy he is using in his YouVersion Bible app is clicking "Read More."

When you tap that, you'll be able to read the verse in the context of what is happening and the message of the writer.

Jeff talked about giving God room to work in our lives:

God doesn't need a huge gap to make a huge impact. He wants to just be a part of our lives, but we have to allow Him to do that. God is the only constant; He's never left our side. It's just whether or not we choose to acknowledge His presence and actively show Him that we want to have a relationship with Him.

It's a true blessing to have met Jeff through Instagram after listening to a podcast on 3 of 7 Project, and we've been great friends ever since. After we connected in the fall of 2020, he has connected me with many other people and even brought me into a men's prayer group called Sons of Thunder. The group meets every Wednesday night to discuss the Word of God. Throughout the week, we send Scriptures to one another and pray for anyone who needs support for anything they are going through.

One of the guys in the Sons of Thunder group is Mike Bellini. Mike and I met through Jeff and connected to run the David Goggins 4x4x48 Challenge with three other men (Tanner, Zach, and Dave). The 4x4x48 is 4 miles, every 4 hours for 48 hours straight. All of us held each other accountable by FaceTiming fifteen minutes before each run. Mike, being the leader he is, led the group in communication.

Mike Bellini, The Disciplined Man

Mike explains his journey of becoming a disciplined man and how having specific goals has sharpened not only his body but more importantly his brain:

> For most of my life, I lived like a sprinter. I would set goals, get inspired, and go hard for short periods, often burning out, falling back, and having to restart all over again. It was a pattern of two steps forward, then one, two, or three steps back. It worked for a while until I found myself a couple of steps behind where I wanted to be and unable to move forward again. I was a few pounds overweight and had appeared to maximize my strength and conditioning. Physically, I was simply treading water, trying desperately not to sink.
>
> That is when I read about a push-up challenge, a three-week routine that builds up to one thousand push-ups in a day. Before that, I had never done a lot of push-ups, but I thought, "This challenge will confirm whether the sands of time have caught up to me and if I was truly as strong and fit as I am ever going to get." I wanted to find out once and for all.
>
> After doing push-ups—a lot of push-ups— throughout those three weeks, I was amazed by the strength it built. The previous year had

been a demoralizing period of stagnation. Yet, in three weeks, my hope for a stronger, more energetic, healthier life became a renewed reality—simply by doing push-ups, in increasing amounts, every single day.

Then came a plank challenge. Thousands of people all over the world were joining a one-month commitment to do a "thing" every day of the month. The trick was, whatever you did on day one of the month, you had to multiply by every other day. For me, it was a one-minute plank. So, a one-minute plank on the first day of the month, was a two-minute plank on the second day, all the way up to a thirty-minute plank on the last day. Let me tell you, I hate planks! A one-minute plank was torture, and I signed up to do four hundred sixty-five minutes of planks for an entire month! What was I thinking?

Simply put, I wanted to get over the mental blockade of doing something hard, something I dreaded. How did I get through it? One minute, one day at a time. Suddenly, on day five, a one-minute plank wasn't a big deal anymore. On day ten, a five-minute plank was a new standard. I learned through doing thousands of push-ups and hundreds of minutes of planks that, regardless of how I felt, how tired my arms and legs were, if I could just get myself to start, I would finish.

These challenges radically changed my perception of push-ups and planks and got me curious. What else could I change my perception of?

How about running? I don't use the word "hate" often, but I legitimately hated running about as much as planks. So, I decided it was time to try making friends with it. I ran a quarter of a mile, times the day of the month, every day for an entire month. A quarter of a mile on day one led up to seven and a half miles on day thirty. Before that month, the longest I had ever run at one time was a 5k, and I had only done that a couple of times for charity events.

Next was writing. Twenty-five years ago, I started writing a book, stopped after a few chapters, and swore I would never attempt it again. The process was too long. I was too impatient. It would be a never-ending pursuit for someone like me. However, I had been hit with a burning internal plea to try it again. So, I implemented the one-month strategy to get it started. For the first month, I wrote every day for ten minutes times the day of the month.

Ten minutes on Day 1; three hundred minutes on Day 30. I learned a couple of things from this challenge: (1) There was a sweet spot of writing time, between seventy-five and ninety minutes, when I was at my best. Beyond that length of time, my mind would wander or get tired, and the quality of the result diminished; (2) Doing a thing consistently, with no quit and very little deviation was the key to finishing.

The next month I took a cold shower every day and started doing cold plunges—submerging myself in cold water for two to three minutes. I don't like the cold either. So why did I cold plunge? For both the physical and mental benefits. There are essentially two parts of a cold plunge, a ten-second shock to the body right when you get in (which is not fun at all) followed by a couple of minutes of intense focus on relaxing and becoming one with the cold. The question I learned to ask myself before getting into the frigid water was, "Am I going to forego the physical benefits of this two-minute activity because I am too scared, worried, or hesitant about the initial ten-second shock?" I began to connect that same question to other areas of life—the difficult conversations, decisions, or situations we so often avoid, mostly because of the initial pain of entry.

Lately, I have gone back to push-ups, but not so much to get stronger; rather, as a method to build the habit of consistently getting up early in the morning. The time I get out of bed is the number of push-ups I do in a day. As soon as the alarm goes off, I start thinking about the push-ups and how quickly I can get up to limit the total. As elementary as that sounds, it works!

What have the results been of all these challenges? I did over one hundred thousand push-ups in a year. The following year, I ran over one thousand miles and completed three ultramarathons. I wrote a book and launched a podcast.

I have also learned so much more through the process of building these habits. They not only produce the desired results, but they also extend to other areas of my life. For instance, to get up early consistently, there are certain things I now know that I must do (hydrate, exercise, focus on a reason to get up) and things I can't do (consume sugar after lunch, eat after dinner) the day before. Building the habit of getting up early has made me healthier and helped me cultivate a lifestyle that doesn't require as much sleep as I used to.

A "lifestyle" is exactly what we build through habits. These activities are no longer challenges to conquer or goals to reach; they are what I do.

I do push-ups. I run. I get up early. I eat well and hydrate. I exercise regularly. I embrace the cold. I keep going. It's what I do. One day at a time. Every day.

These lessons learned by Mike are a perfect example of what you need to do to change your lifestyle. As he mentioned, it takes a clear and intentional mindset coupled with a strong Why you are getting out of bed and attacking your objective. My advice would be to focus on one area of your life you want to improve, break it down to what you could accomplish each day, and then execute without excuses. When this strategy is done correctly, you will build consistency and momentum—and the results will follow. Your habits will eventually become your lifestyle.

So get busy now mapping out your next month or months of what you are going to change and don't wait until tomorrow. Success doesn't happen magically. You have to put in the time and commit to being the best. It's a relentless pursuit!

Action Steps:

- Set three alarms, "The Trifecta" of waking up on time: 1) your phone 2) your alarm clock 3) your watch

- Eat less, exercise more. You'll feel at your best physically.

- Do not eat late at night. When you do, your body works harder and does not allow for a restful sleep.

- Write down your to-do list for the next day and then tackle the hardest tasks first.

Chapter 11

Adjust, Adapt, and Win

Those who cannot change their minds cannot change anything.
— *George Bernard Shaw*

In 2020, everyone had a difficult year in teaching because of COVID-19. In-person teaching stopped in the state of Ohio in March, and we had to immediately switch to online learning. Talk about a complete 180! We had to shift from working with students in our classrooms to online instruction, educating through an entirely new platform—and we had to adapt fast.

For the remaining months of the school year, my wife and I both did our best to work with students on Zoom.

This was a very difficult time for my family. My wife is also a teacher, and we have four children. So a typical day had me in the basement in my makeshift office, while she was either on the main floor or in our bedroom when she had class. Three of our kids—then ages ten, eight, and five—had online classes. Our two-year-old had to be watched by either my wife, myself, or our oldest daughter so he wouldn't escape the house or get into something he shouldn't be into. The "school day" started at 7:00 a.m. for our entire family, and we were not finished until the afternoon.

Chaos would be an understatement in describing what went on in our house for the remaining months of the school year. Balancing the education of our children while at the same time "zooming" in with students from our respective schools was extremely stressful. To say any day went smoothly would be a lie. My wife and I did our best to work together and make sure everyone was taken care of on both ends of the screens. We had tension in our relationship as well because life was completely different and arduous. But we adapted to the new environment and made it work, even though we knew it wasn't perfect. We continued doing our best for all of the kids we were teaching and hoped that we would survive each day without one of our kids getting hurt or damaging something in the house.

Up to 2020, our family has taken only one vacation as a family. We were looking forward to a second—finally! —as the school year wound down and summer approached. But everything in the nation was closing down, and we had to cancel our vacation plans. We didn't have a pool to go to, and our local museums were closed as well. We had been thrown another curveball, but we hit it out of the park by doing what we could control. We decided to make every Wednesday "Wilderness Wednesday," and each week, we went to a new park to hike. We played more games at home, did more art projects, and had more bonding time than we will probably have the rest of our lives.

We were thankful that we were together and made the best of the situation. We had family and friends who lived alone and didn't leave their house for months on end. Many of these people struggled with depression because of the lack of the physical presence of others. During this time, my wife's best friend said one day, "What I would give just to give you guys a hug right now!" That statement was powerful because we had that opportunity each day—and we did not take it for granted. We knew that we were blessed to have one another while millions around the country were at home by themselves. It was hard not to see loved ones, especially in my Italian family. Normally, we saw each other almost every weekend.

Life wasn't normal. It was different, not only for us but for everyone. All of us had to make decisions to keep each other safe while this virus halted our normal way of life.

As a coach and teacher, I had to wear a mask at each golf match and school for the entire day (once we were back in school). We went through masks at our house like they were underwear. My wife made a basket for dirty masks to be washed every week. She even went through a period of "mask anxiety" about not having the right one to wear that would allow her to breathe easier, or whether or not the ones she ordered online were the same masks that had worked for her before. Who would have thought that in our lifetime these worries would even cross our minds? Even with these unique and previously unimagined situations, we pushed through and made it work day in and day out.

Don't Let Your Dreams Die

We have a difficult time changing our ways because change disrupts our life. It interrupts our comfort. This is why we often don't venture into the new. Even though we might want to try something new in life, we don't because we know it will take time, discipline, and effort. We'll have to interrupt the comfort of the known to work at adapting to the new. So we back away from change and new—but then we're also backing away from our dreams.

All of us have potential beyond what we can imagine, but any progress toward a dream comes to a screaming halt and our potential is untapped when we are reluctant to adapt to new habits, new thinking, and new behaviors. For example, how many people after high school or college start something new but never finish—or never even begin—the dream they once had when they were younger? I don't know the statistics, but once we start making some money, many people are just content. Content to be comfortable! Those two words should never cross your mind, ever! Being comfortable means there is little to no growth.

~ Think and Absorb ~

What dream did you once have? Was it to become a business owner, a financial broker, a teacher, a coach, a mother, or a father? It's never too late to start. Write down your dream and put it in several places where you'll see it daily. Have your dream physically within sight; have it "looking" at you each day so that you make it a priority to capture this dream.

Go back to Chapter 9 and review the paragraphs on vision and mission statements. Create your own. Once you have your vision, write steps you will have to intentionally take to accomplish this goal. Once those steps are written down, check yourself daily—Are you getting these steps done?

Changing our path comes more easily if we live with the end in mind.

What I mean is this: Fast forward fifty years and play the game of looking back at your life. Ask yourself, *Do I have any regrets? Did I live the life I was supposed to live?*

Sit on these questions. Let them sink in. Then commit to yourself that you are going to change whatever needs to be changed to make a "no-regret life" a reality. **You have so many gifts and talents to offer the world. Get started today, and don't look back!**

Be Consistent with Your Mission

Sometimes you simply have to adapt to things you cannot change. One day I woke up at 5:00 a.m., went downstairs to pray, and then got ready to run for my scheduled miles. As I stepped outside, I looked up at the sky, darkened with gray clouds, and rain began to fall. I went back inside to check the radar to make sure I wasn't going to be stuck in the middle of a thunderstorm. As I looked at my phone, severe thunderstorm alerts were flaring up. Decision time. Go back inside, relax, and wait for the rain to pass? I think not!

Instead, I decided to ride my bike inside and do my weight-training exercises. After 45 minutes had passed, I reassessed the situation outside. It was still raining, but according to the radar, the thunderstorms had passed. Now was my moment to head out to accomplish what I had intended to do from the beginning.

During the run, I couldn't help but think about how my "old self" would have made a quick decision to not work out at all, and I'd have found something else to do like watching YouTube videos or checking out the scene on Instagram. Some things, like thunderstorms, are out of our control, but we can still make progress toward our goals by going another route. Having a mindset that focuses on the goal will help us adapt and maintain the consistency needed for success.

Consistency means that your daily choices and actions are in line with your vision and mission. My new vision for my life includes running. When I couldn't run in a thunderstorm, my choice as to what I would do with that time was *consistent* with my vision. Unable to go down the usual path (running), I chose to use that time to exercise a little differently. But I did not choose a path (sitting with social media) that was of no benefit to or support of my vision. Consistency with your vision while adapting to new situations will help you make progress in your life as well as influence others in the process.

When I stepped down from the head baseball coach position, I still wanted to continue the Thursday leadership classes that I started as a coach. I asked my administration if I could open the class to the entire student body (I was still pursuing my mission, but adapting.) They loved the idea and said, "Go for it!"

I reached out to our high school coaches and teachers, asking for names of players and students who were leaders in their environment. Those students received a letter welcoming them into the leadership class, and we began the 2020 fall class with ten students in Zoom sessions on Thursday nights. During these classes, we had meaningful discussions on books they read (such as *Extreme Ownership* and *Old School Grit*) and the lessons they learned from the books and one another. Participants in the class were also asked to write down three goals they wanted to accomplish by the end of the year.

We also had six athletes/professionals from around the nation as guests on our Zoom calls. Most of them were ultra-endurance athletes, and we learned about each individual and their success in life. One of our guests was a recovering alcoholic, another had overcome obesity, and the others were business owners who gave the group valuable information on reassessing and reflecting on everything you do daily. Pivoting on things that work and adapting to situations and people was a common theme. We would be up on Zoom for hours, listening to their stories and learning how they had become the man or woman they are today.

All of these lessons were valuable. Success leaves clues, and one word stuck out during our leadership calls: *adapt.* These guest speakers had to adapt to a new lifestyle to become who they are today. There will always be fear of the unknown and the unpredictable future, but knowing what your vision and mission are in life will give you a foundation for dealing with whatever the unknown turns out to be.

If you don't change to new environments or situations, true growth will most likely not occur. A wise man once told me, "Dinosaurs were the strongest animals on Planet Earth at one time, but they didn't adapt to their environment, and therefore, they perished." He used this example to illustrate his point that if you don't adapt to your new place of employment, new situations in life, or changes in a relationship, your environment can consume you with stress and anxiety, and you are going to suffer a great and slow death in your profession or your relationship

Great individuals adapt, average to below-average people do not. Many don't adapt because they are stubborn and set in their ways. They have the fixed mindset that they know how to "do it best," or they think that without them, the company or their family couldn't possibly survive. Success won't become a reality for these people; their pride gets in their way.

Others see adapting as making decisions that will lower their value or compromise their standards or integrity. Instead, think of adapting as learning and growing for the greater good. If for some reason you tried something new in your life and it didn't work, it may be time to plant new seeds to nurture growth.

The best part is, we always have an option to make a change, especially in America. Whether we do or do not change is our choice.

Adjust, adapt, and win in your life.

Action Steps:

- Learn how to adapt to a new business by asking questions

- Learn more skills to benefit your company or family. Being resourceful will help you in each area of your life.

Chapter 12

The Power of One

At 211 degrees, the water is hot. At 212 degrees, it boils. And with boiling water, comes steam. And with steam, you can power a train. ***One extra degree makes all the difference.***

— *Sam Parker*

My friend Bree, who you met in Chapter 6 with her "Teacup Theory" for relationships, also had great advice on how to become a one-percenter in your life. Bree had recently become a mother and was sitting in her office late at night and picked up the magazine, *The Runner's World.* As she was flipping through, she saw a little blurb stating that less than one percent of people in this world will ever complete a marathon. The article was written by a man who explained how he kept putting off his dream of running a marathon; and then one day after an accident, he became paralyzed and couldn't achieve this dream of his.

Growing up, Bree was always active. Her parents put her in gymnastics because she needed to be active in sports.

She still needs this today. Many people don't know what to do after their high school athletic careers have passed, but Bree knew she needed to do *something*. She needed a challenge that would spark her drive again.

After reading that article about the man who talked about running a marathon and then became paralyzed and could not run, Bree's immediate thought was that she had to run a marathon because she may never get the chance again. She wanted to be a part of the one-percent community. Immediately after reading the article, she signed up for a marathon in June and had 6 months to prepare for it. She researched plans on how to run a marathon and stuck to the script, one day at a time. Six months later, she completed her first marathon.

She had found that challenge she needed. For twenty-plus years now, she has been running races. Recently, a shift occurred for her. She wanted to do more than just marathons. One day she was listening to Chadd Wright on the *Rich Roll Podcast,* and he talked about growing as an individual by doing hard events and learning more about yourself. Bree knew then that she had a new mission: "Constantly look for growth in everything." She was drawn to Chadd, the founder of the 3 of 7 Project. She wanted to meet him and find out how he tapped into the power of strength and conquest.

She applied for one of the basic courses that he offers. The course description is one single sentence about what will occur: *The Basic Course is a multi-day experience spent in the wilderness where you will not only learn backpacking skills but also how to become the most complete version of yourself.* She applied, she got accepted, and participated in the Basic Course in March of 2021. She, Jeff Forrester, and seven other men, along with their leaders (Chadd, Blake, and Nate), went on a weekend backpacking trip to recalibrate their Why. She learned during this course how to be more intentional in every aspect of her life and why she should step up her game to do more bold events.

2021 was a banner year for Bree. She completed many ultra events, including one in which she climbed the height of Mount Everest—that's 29,029 feet—in less than 36 hours! She explained why she started to explore this arena of athletics. There are so many variables that you cannot control, such as the weather or how your body will respond to the course or the extra miles. **The one thing you can control is your day-to-day preparation mentally and physically for each event. You need to have a strong Why and be supported along the way by your family and friends.**

Bree is a model of what it takes to be a one-percenter in life. You have to live life boldly, be intentional in your actions, and have a strong Why for doing events in your life.

We only get *one* shot at this life. Why be average? Stop now, and think about something you want to achieve. Then set a date on your calendar to accomplish that goal.

~ *Think and Absorb* ~

Stacking One Brick at a Time

Sticking to a plan, being intentional, and always striving to achieve goals has made me a one-percenter in life. Things aren't always easy, but since I stuck to the plan of running my marathons, even during COVID and when races were canceled, I was able to develop relationships with individuals I learned about via podcasts. If it wasn't for that lonely marathon I ran that day, I would not have met Jeff, who led me to Bree, Chas Allen, Rob Matthews, Mike Bellini, and so many more. These doors of relationships would never have been opened if I had not stuck to my plan of running the race on the date that was set.

Staying on a schedule each day has a major impact on your results in life. For example, I have learned to do just one task per day in each area of my life to help me grow. My one-per-day habits include: one prayer when I rise, sharing one Bible verse on social media, one mile each day, one contact with another person, at least one "I love you," one new piece of information learned.

The power of one-per-day can also be applied to achieving something per week or even per month, like writing one thank-you card per week or going on one date per month. I have learned that if you break down your habits into "ones," you stack bricks of success. Many people have not learned this concept of breaking down goals into simple steps. Some individuals may feel that goals or new habits are hard to achieve because they either have a lack of confidence to start them or are not disciplined enough to be consistent. To start moving toward your goals, let's look at how this can be achieved by breaking down the concept visually.

Think of stacking one brick at a time. If you were to stack one brick at a time, each day, you will eventually build a mighty fortress. To build a castle and the surrounding fortress, imagine how many bricks you would have to stack in your lifetime. But by being consistent and stacking more bricks each day and never taking a day off, your castle is built! **In the same way, it is possible to build your legacy, and it starts with just one brick.**

Your castle should not be just of the flesh, just earthly, but it should be built for the True Kingdom, for eternity. Luke 12:32 states, "Do not be afraid, little flock, for your Father has been pleased to give you the Kingdom." The power of influencing just one person at a time by imitating Christ and sharing the Gospel with them is what the essence of life is truly all about. There is no better person to illustrate this story than my friend Rob, who went to the pits of hell and back. He is having a major impact by making one decision—to live for others.

Rob's Transformation

Rob, who I met through Jeff Forrester, talked to me on my podcast about his transformation from anxiety and depression to having freedom and peace of mind. His story began in 2017, when his depression and anxiety was at its worst. He was driving to work one day and felt terrible; things just didn't seem right. He called his dad and tried to describe how he felt. "I feel like I'm dying," he said. He tells his story:

> I decided not to go to the hospital and went to the store to pick up some supplies. When I got there, I had the same feeling, pain in my chest, and an overwhelming sense of fear. What was happening was I was having a panic attack.
>
> The next day, I had a meeting with my paint sales representative and during our conversation, I left mid-conversation and went home. I went home, lay on the couch, and decided to take the rest of the week off work. The first week off, I just read and lay around. I was still getting that feeling once in a while. These panic attacks were more frequent during the day, and as weeks passed, I got to the point where I couldn't even go out my front door. I couldn't leave my house, and I became housebound, and when my kids left for school, I would slink downstairs and just read and sleep.
>
> During this time, I tried to alleviate my depression and anxiety by reading the Bible every day. I was very obsessive about getting to know God. The mistake I made during this time was trying to make God a magic wand. I became obsessed with filling my day with

everything about God, including music and books. I studied all I could and was hoping He'd fix my problem, but I never started a relationship with Him.

I didn't pray; instead, I was on an intellectual journey to God.

About four months into this deep dive of depression and trying to have God fix my problem, I woke up one night around 2:00 a.m. My daughter was at her mother's house, since we were divorced, and I decided that tonight I would kill myself. So I started researching the best way to do it without making it a gruesome scene for anyone who found me.

As I was Googling how to commit suicide, an ad came up with a suicide hotline to call. I decided that I would call them to give them a piece of my mind; I was not looking for support to change the outcome I wanted. I talked to the specialist on the line for about twenty minutes, and then after I got off the phone, I suddenly realized that I wanted to help others who were thinking about committing suicide. I went to sleep shortly after coming to this realization and woke up the next morning with a new purpose.

This new purpose was to help others and give them hope. To do this, I needed to get into a routine to get my life back on track and have some consistency. I needed to start doing something physical every day if I was going to get my body and mind right. So I decided to order a treadmill and just slowly begin walking each day. Before the treadmill was delivered, I started to walk outside in my cul-de-sac. The path was only a couple of minutes long, and to paint a picture of how bad I still was, some days I had my wife come and get me because I couldn't move. Then my wife started to follow me in her car on the walk just to help me get through it.

Once the treadmill came in, I began to run again. I would run the first thirty seconds, walk for two minutes, and continue this for a duration of time. I would do this for three or four days and then not touch running for a couple of weeks.

Then one day I read a forum about a lady who was depressed and had such bad anxiety that she hadn't left her home for over thirty years! After I read about this lady, I committed that I did not want to end up like her.

I started to hit the treadmill each day, and I just committed to making small progress, one day at a time. I started to record each day how many kilometers I did on the treadmill, and then one night decided to go outside for a run. This was the first time in many months that I had gone outside. I got home, and I woke up my wife with excitement, telling her that I just completed a 5k. **This one moment of triumph changed my trajectory, getting me back on track.** My efficacy started to increase and I started to believe in myself again. Physical transformation took place as well as spiritual enlightenment.

I started to talk to Jesus and build a relationship with Him. I started reading my books, and as I began this journey again of searching for knowledge, I had a change in my heart that I needed to stop seeking information and just trust to build a relationship. Then I read Isaiah 40:31 and Matthew 11:28, which both refer to being renewed with strength, having persistence, and having the Lord carry the burden. By reading the Word each day and meditating on it, Scripture started to become warm hugs of comfort for me instead of just information about God.

As I started to build a relationship with Christ, I started to go back to work, one day at a time, and just focused on the presence of what I was doing at work and on getting to build a relationship with God. What I learned during this course of events was that I was very thankful for this journey of having my panic attacks occur if it led me to a transformation in my life, which was to live for Christ and offer people hope.

Rob's story teaches us that even depression and anxiety, which equated to suffering, was a gift and not a punishment. This suffering allowed him to find his purpose in life, which is to give people hope each day. Every day he shares Bible verses, music, videos, or just words of encouragement to friends or people he just met on social media. His mission is to help one person get out of their hole of depression and give them the wisdom to understand how to get out—which is to find peace in Christ and have a purpose to help others.

You may be dealing with some internal or external struggles, or you may be closely connected to someone who is suffering in this way. Rob had to experience the lowest point of his life to have an awakening to his purpose. Hopefully, you don't have to reach that point, and reading this book can provide a ray of light that will help you get out of your rut by just starting to do something small, one step at a time, to help yourself mentally, physically, and spiritually. Also, never be afraid to contact one person, just like Rob did, to help you get back on track and live the life you were destined to live.

From Average to Powerhouse Athlete

Around 6 a.m. on a solo early morning run at a local metro park, I met a group of three people running up a steep hill. As I passed them and their headlamps beamed in my eyes, I said, "Hello," and I thought, *Are these people crazy for being out here this early? Wait a minute, I must be crazy as well.*

As my run progressed, I passed the three runners on a loop an hour or so later and asked if I could join them. They politely said yes, and that began the formation of a strong relationship with Jen, DeQuan, and Sam. That one run changed my routine of running solo; one question led to my now running with them every weekend.

Jen Collister is the leader of the group. She sends a text midweek telling us where and when to meet. I look forward to "the text" because I can't wait to see where we'll be meeting to enjoy a "therapy run" together.

I mentioned Jen in Chapter 6, which discussed the importance of surrounding yourself with great people. I can think of no better example of someone who has built momentum one step at a time to become a one-percenter than Jen. It's simply remarkable how she became a "powerhouse athlete." She was not athletically inclined as a kid. She didn't play sports in high school either. In college, she lifted some weights and took some step classes, but that was the extent of her physical activity.

When Jen and her husband separated, her life shifted and she began to build an impressive resume of races and triathlons—one step at a time.

It began when she joined the Cleveland Athletic Club (CAC) and started working with her friend Nicole, who was a runner. Nicole wanted to turn Jen into her running partner, so she patiently worked with Jen every week, chatting with her as she tried to breathe while responding, since the training was intense. Jen trained for and ran her first 5k in 2001, when she was almost 30. It was awful, Jen recalls, and she almost threw up at the end.

Her goal the following year was to get faster at the 5k, but fate intervened in the form of Shannon, a CAC friend. Not only did Shannon convince Jen to join a summer rowing league, but she talked Jen into doing her first triathlon even though Jen didn't know how to swim and didn't own a bike. Jen was convinced to compete; she trained and finished the Cleveland Triathlon in downtown Cleveland, swimming near the Rock Hall of Fame in aqua shoes, biking on a hybrid bike on the Shoreway, and running/walking on the downtown streets. For those who aren't in the triathlon world, Jen used highly ineffective equipment. During the entire event, she was swearing she'd ever do this again, but after she crossed the finish line, she was hooked.

One Race at a Time

Jen had her sights on a marathon. She also started dating Matt, a triathlete she had recently met. Knowing Matt and the other triathletes made her think that she could complete longer distance triathlons as well. She did the Olympic-distance (.9-mile swim, 24.8-mile bike, 10k run) Greater Cleveland Triathlon in 2004. She also trained for and completed the Chicago marathon in October 2004, with a time of 5 hours and 15 minutes. After completing longer distances, she swore again that she would never do another one. Spoiler alert: That promise wasn't kept, but it did take a while for anyone to talk her into another race.

Not long after this race, Jen hired a coach and began training for a full Ironman-distance race. She was committed to completing the race and trained hard each day to make this become a reality. A full Ironman includes a 2.4-mile swim, 112-mile bike ride, and then a marathon (26.2 miles) to finish the race. Her overall time was 15:52:33. She had hoped and trained for a better time but was so proud to have completed an Ironman—something that .01 percent of people will ever do in their life.

After this race, her focus turned toward her family. Eventually, she closed the door on triathlons (although she did do a half-Ironman when her son was 14 months old), and new opportunities opened up.

Jen just turned 50, and 20 years after she started competing in races, she has completed her goal of doing two weekends of all three distances in Spartan Races. While grueling, they still didn't measure up to the caliber of an Ironman, so Jen doubts she will have a Spartan tattoo to match her Ironman one.

She doesn't know what the future holds but hopes she can continue to find a worthy goal (maybe a BHAG) each year, have fun with her friends, and age gracefully. She finished our conversation about her successes by stating:

> I get my workout done every single morning because I know I might not have time for it later, and I can get it done most of the time while my kids are still asleep. It gets my day started right and doesn't leave any lingering stress about that hanging over my head. I work out with friends when possible to enjoy their company while getting my workout completed. I sign up for goal races to keep me honest and "on plan." It also helps that I have a coach who keeps me accountable with assigned daily workouts, but that is quite a privilege most won't have.

One Decision

Jen's passion for our running group to get together each weekend is a standard she has set. Her consistency to that standard is unparalleled. This most recent Saturday morning, I woke up and looked at the outside temperature; it was one degree Fahrenheit. I was scheduled to run with Jen and DeQuan, and I thought to myself, *Should we go outside today with temps this low?* That one thought of doubt, the temptation to deflect from the plan, popped into my head, but I didn't let my feelings dictate my choice. I met both of them on the run, in freezing temperatures, and we had a blast.

The warmth of the conversation while we ran kept the warmth kindling in our legs, and we laughed about the cold as icicles hung from our beards—well, DeQuan's and mine. **See, the thing is, you can't make memories by doing "average" things.** We could have all stayed at home, done our individual workouts inside, and had a normal day. But that is not what life is about. Life is about exploring, taking that chance, having some risk, and being a part of a group that builds you up.

This changed mindset and new relationships all occurred because I asked one question: "Do you mind if I run with you?" That one question changed the trajectory of how I train on the weekends, but even more important are the friendships I have acquired. **So even if it's one degree outside, do the hike, run your scheduled run, because you never know when that one decision could change your life.**

Action Steps:

- Plan to focus on just one task at a time. 1 Prayer, 1 Text, 1 Thank you, 1 Date, 1 Mile, 1 life you can change!

- Achieve your big goals by stacking one brick at a time.

- Have a plan and then work daily on it.

- Surround yourself with highly focused and competitive individuals.

Chapter 13

The Last Line

Our date of death is not the date etched on our tombstone. The day we stop dreaming is the day we start dying.

— *Mark Batterson*

Reflecting on life and the velocity at which it moves during our existence, we know we have only a short time before the flesh expires. While in this world, we have to raise the next generation with knowledge and wisdom. We must live daily to educate our children, youth, younger co-workers, and everyone whose lives intersect ours, to leave them on a more successful and fortuitous path than we have lived. Our objective, therefore, should be to teach the next generation the methods in which the world operates and how to maximize the gifts they have been given.

As we conclude this journey, I hope you have learned from the stories of many individuals and the specific action steps you can use in your life. Know that you can change and make an impact on your life and others.

Being a teacher, coach, parent, podcaster, and now author, these experiences have taught me that we can have an extreme amount of positive influence in others' lives. To be an agent of change takes daily discipline, intentionality, care, and love for yourself and others. You can accomplish your dreams and influence those you will meet in your life.

Where do we want to work? Who will we marry? How will we raise a family? And what is our mission in life? These questions are not only for teenagers or young adults. No matter our age or experience, we need to always be in pursuit of learning and looking for opportunities where we can grow, prioritizing our time, and being intentional in choices that line up with our mission in life, whatever that may be. **All of us need to surround ourselves with excellent individuals who will help us grow and hold us accountable to be the next best version of ourselves.**

Simply growing older does not always mean we are maturing. But if we want to have influence, we need to be constantly growing mentally, physically, and spiritually, and showing those around us, especially our children, students, and young adults, what it takes to be on a mission, to be a person of character in pursuit of greatness! **As parents, you must show your children these concepts of hard work, communication, and love for others.** We have to take this task seriously—and for the right reasons. Our future and the future of the next generations depend on our guiding them to be a better generation than the one we are living in now. This all takes a genuine and selfless mindset.

An example of the urgency of conveying these messages to youth could not be more properly told than through the story of Michelle, a high school teacher, mother, and loving wife. Michelle and my wife, Megan, worked together in a suburban district on the west side of Cleveland. Michelle was older than my wife and took Megan under her wing when Megan was hired in 2005. Out of the goodness of her heart, Michelle mentored Megan, and they formed a loving and lasting relationship.

More than a mentor, Michelle was a sister and best friend to Megan as she listened to my wife when we began to have children and were going through difficult times at school or at home. Michelle was a great listener and gave words of wisdom to Megan and others in the school. Almost daily on their drive home from school, Michelle and Megan would talk, to decompress and discuss when they needed each other's help in finding clarity on a situation.

This beautiful relationship came to an end in early January of 2020. Michelle was teaching her science class one afternoon when she collapsed to the floor. The class stopped, and the kids in her class reached out for help. Megan quickly heard from another staff member that Michelle had passed out, and she rushed to her room and saw her friend lying on the floor as trained individuals attempted to resuscitate her. Michelle was then rushed to the hospital, where she fought for her life. A couple of days went by, and her condition did not improve. She left this earth on January 11, 2020.

This beautiful, loving friend of my wife will never be able to teach lessons in the classroom again. But she has left a legacy that can teach all of us how to live our lives. She left this earth doing what she did best, teaching with passion while loving others. Michelle's life was filled with giving, sharing, and loving people. She was always calm and confident in herself and shared these principles with those around her daily. We who read or hear her story should look to her example as we strive to live our lives to the fullest.

We must learn from Michelle's story that we are not guaranteed tomorrow and that every day we need to give our best for others. We have an obligation, a duty to support those around us and guide them to knowledge, wisdom, and hope for their future. **Each day is a gift, given to us so we can give to others.** We are the last line of defense! The next generation needs us to be our best each day, to share our talents, and to show them what a man or woman of character looks like daily.

Who is molding the youth of our society now? Who is teaching them to work and be contributing members of society? Are they learning what it takes to build a strong family unit?

~ Think and Absorb ~

I have concluded that I can only control what I can control. I used to listen to the mainstream media or YouTube figureheads and just take in content like a four-course meal for my brain. The only problem was, I didn't do anything to make a difference. In my head, I thought that I was making a difference by listening to what was going on or what might happen in the future. I have now turned off those channels and have been doing two specific things per day that I know I can control: stop listening to mainstream media and start being positive support to my community.

How do we take action to support those around us? Some of the easy ways could simply be donating your time to a school, your church, or your community. Most of these institutions would not turn you away if you offer to provide your experience to children or adults. **To make a difference, we have to be agents of change. We can't complain or point fingers. We must take action!**

Trimming the fat off our lives and focusing on the substance of what matters to us will help us stay driven and have a purpose in life. Being extremely intentional about what we want to achieve, having a vision, and writing down non-negotiable tasks will allow us to make progress toward our goals; but more importantly, we'll promote growth in other lives as well. With these concepts in place in our lives and having tasks we do daily, we'll see the outcomes we want.

Case in point, I made a conscious decision to write each day for ten minutes. I wasn't perfect every day, but I was very aware that this task was part of my vision, my mission, and my opportunity to change lives by sharing the lessons illustrated in the lives of people I have met. I included many stories not just for the sake of storytelling but to gain knowledge from these experiences. You have gained something that helps you with your mission in life, and you can then help others around you as well.

See the Mission Through

Finish strong with what you've started. See the mission through. You'll have to adjust along the way, you'll adapt, and you'll still win if you stay consistent in your mission.

I met Connor and his family when he entered high school as a freshman. I would see him in the hallways and classes leading up to his first season as a baseball player in my program. I remember his parents being very supportive in their emails and conversations with me when they came to pick him up. Connor's love for baseball was secondary to hockey since he had family members who played professionally. Nonetheless, I knew that he liked baseball and was a great kid.

In Connor's first season, he played JV as a pitcher, catcher, shortstop, and sometimes outfielder. As a sophomore, he played similar roles on the varsity squad. There was something about Connor that was special. He showed up every day, never complained, and was a quiet leader who led by example. I loved coaching him because of his winning attitude and his work ethic. He was also smart, reflective, and aware of situations on and off the field.

When his sophomore season was coming to an end, my tenure as the head varsity coach was coming to a halt as well. This decision didn't come easily, and Connor was one specific player I didn't want to let down. I loved coaching him and wanted to see him progress, not only as a player but as a person.

After I announced my decision in May of 2019, as tears rolled from my eyes, I embraced many players and families. During my farewell speech, my wife texted me—and I knew I had made the right decision in resigning. The text informed me that my son had just hit his first home run. The thought of missing my children's successes and experiences outweighed my desire to coach. This was not selfish but selfless; I was moving forward with my time and commitment to my family.

Months passed, and the 2020 spring baseball season was around the corner. I was eager to help sporadically with anything the new coach needed. I didn't want to step on any toes, so I didn't help when the practices started. I was excited about watching some games, but then COVID-19 spawned its ugly terror across the nation. The 2020 spring season was canceled.

When spring rolled around again in 2021, things were almost back to normal. February, when baseball would begin, was upon us, and I always checked in with my former players to see how they were doing. I did not help with practice but was there for them to support their season and success.

One day I observed a person walking into school on crutches. Lo and behold, it was Connor.

I immediately went to talk to him and asked what had happened. He told me he had collided with another hockey player over the weekend, and he had a fractured femur and a slight tear in his meniscus. He would have to have surgery, but there was a chance for him to come back during the middle of the baseball season.

I took this as my opportunity to be there for him, to help him be ready if there was a chance for him to play during the season. I told Connor that I would play catch with him after school and throw him ground balls. He was ecstatic that I would take the time to help him. I did it because I love the kid. He gave me joy when I was around him. I also wanted to be there to give him that fighting chance to be game-ready once he was cleared to play.

We worked after school a couple of days of the week; he sat on a chair and we threw a ball back and forth. Days turned into weeks, and the crutches and knee brace were removed. He regained strength and mobility and slowly worked himself back into the lineup by April.

The joy I felt to be part of his progress cannot be described. My cup overflowed with gratitude to see him return to baseball. I had a different role now, but my mission remained the same: to help boys become men, on and off the diamond.

Connor returned, and on senior night, under the lights, with bases loaded, he had a walk-off hit to win the game against a formidable opponent. I wasn't there, but I heard the kids telling the story the next day and saw their glowing faces as they talked about how it felt to win that game.

The next week, I was there in person to watch Connor and his fellow players win their first playoff game. I witnessed growth and maturity from so many of my former players. I also had former students and players greet me and talk at great length about their lives. These conversations, coupled with hugs and true enjoyment of being in the presence of one another, made a resounding impact on my heart. I knew that I had made a difference in their lives—because they told me. These players and other former students had written me letters and given me cards to show their appreciation of my determination to see them succeed in life.

Being There for Others

On January 21, 2022, I got a text from Scott, a new friend in my 40 Days of Deliverance program. His text said "I need prayer for my brother Andy. It's bad and I'm scared." I replied that I would be praying, and then twenty minutes later he texted again: "I love you, John. Unfortunately, my brother passed away."

I was at a standstill when I read those words. I didn't know many details of the situation, but I did know that his brother was not that old. I couldn't imagine losing my brother, especially one who is a best friend and loved dearly. After praying and contacting Chas, a friend who is close to Scott, all we could do was support him. I continued to pour out my thoughts, prayers, and communication to support Scott the only way I knew how, by loving him. **Love is the only way to show the heart of Christ and the essence of who God is.**

Everyone in the 40 Days of Deliverance group reached out to Scott by phone, texting, gifts, and other ways. In just 20 days of the program, we had formed a true sense of fellowship with one another. There is no better way to explain the true source of fellowship than these words from 1 John 1:1-7.

> That which was from the beginning, which we have heard, which we have seen with our eyes, which we have looked at and our hands have touched—this we proclaim concerning the Word of life. The life appeared; we have seen it and testify to it, and we proclaim to you the eternal life, which was with the Father and has appeared to us. We proclaim to you what we have seen and heard, so that you also may have fellowship with us. And our fellowship is with the Father and with his Son, Jesus Christ. We write this to make our joy complete. This is the message we have heard from him and declare to you: God is light; in him, there is no darkness at all. If we claim to have fellowship with him and yet walk in the darkness, we lie and do not live out the truth. But if we walk in the light, as he is in the light, we have fellowship with one another, and the blood of Jesus, his Son, purifies us from all sin.

To understand how to truly have meaningful relationships with others, we need to connect daily with the holiness of God, the Son, and the Holy Spirit (the Trinity). When we learn from the Trinity, we can imitate Their ways and show how to love, be a comforter, and be a light to others.

Taking action to love others and support them in their journey is a mission for all of us.

Scott's brother Andy had wanted to join the group in the summer session. The love of Christ flowing through the fellowship of the 40 Days group impacted Scott so powerfully that he wanted his brother to feel that same sense of fellowship and love, which he had never really experienced before. Scott buried his brother Andy in the 40 Days T-shirt that he received the week after his brother's passing. He didn't want his brother to miss out on the love that he felt.

Our mission in life is to impact people with such conviction of love that they couldn't imagine being separated from it. That is how God loves us. His love is unconditional, without strings attached, a pure love that can only be felt when you completely surrender your will to His will and trust in His plans for you.

Planting seeds for the harvest

My mission is to serve the Lord and imitate His ways while exhausting all of my gifts for His Kingdom. In this mission, I plan on being a light-bearer and give people hope for their futures. To do that, I have to plant daily seeds of life by my words, actions, and interactions.

The stories in this book remind us that our actions impact people every day, for the better or the worse. **With our words and actions, we can build people up to be their best or tear them down with discouragement and negativity. We have a choice.**

Bringing change to our country and our world starts with us being role models, teachers, coaches, and parents. We can't give up on others or pass the buck to someone else. It is our responsibility to make the change.

We are the last line of defense! We have the gifts and talents to help those around us. There is no other way around it. We have the opportunity each day to help others be better. We can't make excuses anymore that "this is the way this generation is" or "they just don't get it." We have to sharpen their awareness of potential so they know they can be great individuals, contributors to society, and people who will make an impact in our world. All of us need to do our part, our duty, to teach our kids, our students, or our younger co-workers how to be responsible and caring people. We need to show them what hard work is and how they can achieve greatness with a positive mindset and continuous pursuit of their craft.

> Help people maximize their God-given potential. Potential is God's gift to us; what we do with it is our gift back to God. Helping people maximize their God-given potential is why God put me on this planet. That is what gets me up early and keeps me up late. Nothing is more exhilarating to me than seeing people grow into their God-given giftedness. -- Mark Batterson

If you feel as though you don't have a skill set or the personality to help someone else, simply learn from others who are successful. Read their books, watch their interviews on YouTube, or follow them on social media.

Turn off the negativity and start making a difference in someone else's life. I promise that once you make this change, you will not only feel better but you will begin making a profound impact at home, work, and your community.

Be an active agent of change by continually growing as a person. By doing so, you will be able to influence others along the way and create a loving fellowship with many people in your community—and possibly the world! Make these changes today, offer people your gifts, and live a life full of love and support for others.

Be the person everyone deserves in their lives.

Start your new business, write your book, and passionately pursue a job that you love. While you pursue your passions, influence others positively, share your gifts, continually grow in wisdom, and never forget that you are and will always be loved by God. This world needs you to maximize your talents, show others how to be a person of action, and show genuine love for everyone.

You have what it takes. Just trust in the Lord, and He will deliver you!

Action Steps:

- Don't judge a book by its cover.

- Tell the truth to our young adults, but teach them how to be successful with the gifts that they have.

- Be a Michelle to everyone in your life.

- Be an agent of change by action for your family, community, and country.

- Teach people to live life, with a full commitment and love for them.

- Share your gifts with others.

- Be a beacon of hope and light to others, and live a legacy of service.

Acknowledgments

This book would not have been possible if it weren't for my family. I have the most profound respect for my parents (Tom and Susan), grandparents, wife (Megan), brothers (Todd, James), sister (Rachel), and children (Giuliana, Benjamin, Calvin, and Elijah). Solid families like the one I grew up in and that my wife and I have also established create an environment of hope, love, peace, and joy. Learning these daily behaviors as I grew up, along with being taught to respect and love my neighbor, developed my character. The foundation was laid for me, and I am blessed to have the opportunity now, in this book, to use my God-given talents to tell stories and offer lessons that will impact many lives.

Individuals besides my family who have helped me are Gail Michalski (former supervisor), Larry Logan (middle school history teacher), Bob Ritley (high school football coach), Mike Ryan (high school baseball coach), Jeff Hartmann (high school baseball coach), Bonnie Kovacic (teacher), Michelle Carino (teacher), Lisa Shields (supervisor), and many others.

I also want to thank all of my coaches, teachers, priests, mentors, and groups of people with whom I've had relationships over the years, both in the past and in the present. Each person has helped to mold me into the person I have become. These influential people have allowed me to grow as an individual, and without this circle of motivating, humble, and loving people, this book may not have gotten into your hands today.

Dominic Ianiro helped with the first phase of editing this manuscript. Elaine Starner spent countless hours swiftly editing and making this book the finished product it is today. She truly is an expert in her craft. Along this journey we forged a great friendship that will never be forgotten. Dominick Domasky, my publisher, challenged me to push my boundaries and think outside the box. His support and resourcefulness have helped me to keep motivating others through multiple platforms and experiences. I also want to thank Chris Fabish for his hard work and skills for the creation of the cover for the book. Chris is an amazing man with so much talent!

Lastly, but most importantly, the beloved Trinity (God, Jesus, and the Holy Spirit). Without the blessings given to me by the Triune God, none of this would have been possible.

About the Author

John Grdina is a special education teacher, leadership coach, and podcast host. He has taught in public education for the past seventeen years, including career and technical education, where he began his career. He is the coordinator of an international program, coaches multiple sports, and teaches a leadership class at his school. His first book, *Freedom to Ascend,* brings his knowledge and experiences together to show there is hope where many think there is none.

John graduated from John Carroll University in 2004 with a Bachelor of Arts degree, earned his Master's in Education in 2009 from Notre Dame College, and his Education Innovation and Leadership endorsement in 2019 from Fort Hays State University. In his spare time, he is an ultra-endurance athlete who helps train other athletes across the United States, the owner of a TrueSupporter Group that prays for those in need, and the founder of 40 Days of Deliverance, a program to improve individuals in mind, body, and spirit.

John currently lives in Cleveland Heights, Ohio, with his wife (Megan) and four children (Giuliana, Benjamin, Calvin, and Elijah). In his leisure time, he enjoys nature walks with his family, coaching and supporting his children's local sports teams, and spending time with his extended family. He loves helping others grow and wants everyone to "exhaust all their gifts" that God has given them.

If you are interested in a true transformation in your life or company, John can be reached for coaching, consulting, keynotes, and media appearances at grdinajohn@gmail.com.

If you want to view more of John's work, programs, or social media, simply scan the QR code below:

How to scan the QR code:

1. Open the camera app
2. Focus the camera on the QR code by gently tapping the code
3. Follow the instructions on the screen to complete the action

CPSIA information can be obtained
at www.ICGtesting.com
Printed in the USA
BVHW040849250422
635249BV00016B/431